SCHOOL OF BACH-PLAYING
FOR THE ORGANIST

General Editor: GORDON PHILLIPS

VOLUME TWO

SCHOOL OF BACH-PLAYING FOR THE ORGANIST

General Editor: GORDON PHILLIPS

VOLUME TWO

Bach's Organ-Registration

by

WILLIAM L. SUMNER

HINRICHSEN EDITION LTD.

Bach House, 10-12 Baches Street
London, N.1

Peters Edition House, 38 Berners Street
London, W.1

373 Park Avenue South, New York 16, N.Y.

SOLE AGENTS:
C. F. PETERS CORPORATION
373 Park Avenue South
New York, N. Y. 10016

SCHOOL OF BACH-PLAYING FOR THE ORGANIST

A series of guide books and music, covering various aspects of organ-playing
as applicable to the works of J. S. Bach

General Editor: Gordon Phillips

ARTICULATION IN ORGAN PLAYING**

A " Little Organ Book " for Manuals only, based on 31 Chorale Preludes and
Chorales by Bach, arranged in the order of the Liturgical Year
by Gordon Phillips, with a Foreword by Robert Donington

BACH'S ORGAN-REGISTRATION†

All Chorale Prelude Titles in German and English
The BWV Numbering—The Nicknamed Organ Works
by William L. Sumner, with a Foreword by Ivor Keys

TEMPO AND RHYTHM IN BACH'S ORGAN MUSIC†

by Robert Donington, with a Foreword by Gordon Phillips

BACH'S ART OF PART-PLAYING*

A collection of six short Trios with advice on registration and method of study
by Stainton de B. Taylor

BACH'S METHOD OF TRIO-PLAYING**

The 2-part Inventions, arranged as Trios, with a third part added by Max Reger
and Karl Straube (not for U.S.A. and Canada)

BACH'S ART OF FUGUE*

The complete work laid out for the organ in an eminently practical manner,
by Hans Schuricht

FIGURED BASS BACH STUDIES*

Bach's 69 Sacred Songs and Arias from " Schemelli's Musicalisches Gesangbuch
of 1736 " are among the most beautiful religious music. They offer the greatest
possible inspiration to those who are working on the realisation of figured bass.
The melodies are printed in the soprano clef and the basses left just as Bach wrote
them. Most suitable for practice besides the mechanical exercises offered in
text-books. (Peters Edition No. 4573)

(further volumes in preparation)

*—music.   †—book.   **—text and music.

PRINTED IN ENGLAND BY
ROBERT STOCKWELL LTD., LONDON, S.E.1

CONTENTS

5

FOREWORD

THE LAST FEW decades have seen a gradual erosion of romantic fallacies about the nature of the organ. The nineteenth-century notion of "bigger and better" has given way before a growing suspicion that the undoubted pinnacle of organ composition – J. S. Bach's work – was contemporary with the pinnacle of organ design, and that the one cannot be properly understood without a clear understanding of the other. "Back to Bach" as a slogan has had to cover some ludicrous notions of composition in the twentieth century, but as far as organs go it has much to recommend it. This change of opinion has been fostered by the insistent efforts of a number of writers, amongst whom Dr. Sumner is distinguished by his constant appeal to facts – of which he seems to have a far greater store than most people. But "revolution" is perhaps too strong a word for an untidy situation. Enthusiasts without real knowledge have built organs which would have made Bach scream, and some organists feel that they have done their duty by eschewing the swell pedal and drawing 8 ft. and 2 ft. stops without regard to their voicing.

It is vital that every organist should know the contents of this book. The first-hand evidence of Bach's registration is sparse (it is all here), but the practice of organ-builders and organists of the early eighteenth century is well-documented, and this book is so to speak a distillation of a sea of knowledge in which the less learned are apt to get out of their depth. Let not the possessor of a hopelessly unsuitable instrument feel that it is not for him. The insight he will receive should make him a better Bach player, and that should surely be the object of any organist worth the name.

IVOR KEYS

PREFATORY NOTE

I AM most grateful to Professor Ivor Keys, M.A., D.Mus., F.R.C.O., for writing such an excellent foreword to this small work, and also to him and Gordon Phillips for their patience in reading the manuscript carefully and making some helpful suggestions.

W.L.S.

PART ONE

BACH'S ORGAN-REGISTRATION

THE GERMAN ORGAN IN BACH'S TIME

J. S. BACH left very few indications concerning the organ stops which were to be used in playing his works; and even such registration directions as he gave have been the subject of some controversy.

Before we consider the markings on Bach's scores or copies thereof, it is necessary to understand the nature of the German organ of his day and the stops which constituted its tonal resources. Bach lived in a time of change as far as organ design was concerned. The period of high baroque in organ design had waned before his death in 1750. Moreover, the ideals and methods of the notable schools of organ-builders differed in various parts of Germany. Bach was associated in one way or another with the organs in Thuringia, the central " greenheart " of Germany, the organs in and around Leipzig and the Hanseatic organs of the Schnitger School in Lübeck, Hamburg and Lüneberg. The organs built by Arp Schnitger (1648-1719) and his school were the typical organs of the baroque period in North Germany, and they were all built according to certain principles of tonal and physical structure. The latter was most important, and it is useless to consider the nature of the individual ranks of organ pipes, and the methods of combining them, until there is an understanding of the disposition of the various sections of the organ in relation to one another and to the building in which the organ was placed.

The organ was placed on a gallery backed by a wall. Usually the gallery was the highest available, and sometimes was very high, as in the Duke's Chapel at Weimar. The main organ (Hauptwerk) was contained in the main-case, in the lower part of which were the keyboards and stops. On each side of the case were towers, which contained the large pedal pipes and behind them the smaller pedal pipes. In a smaller case, behind the back of the player, and hence called Rück-positiv (positive organ at the back) was the second most important manual division. Its number of stops and power were comparable with those of the Hauptwerk. This division was nearer to the congregation than any other part of the organ. In a three-manual organ, the third manual was known as *Brust-werk* (breast work). Although some imaginative organ-builders divided it into two parts and placed it on each side of the key-boards, the usual place for this section was immediately above the music desk and just below the Hauptwerk. This smaller section of the instrument could be closed by cupboard doors, and its pipes could easily be reached by the organist. Since it contained ranks of regal pipes which easily went out of tune, its ready accessibility to the organist was an advantage, indeed, a necessity. A fourth manual section could take the shape of another smaller section placed above the pipes of the Hauptwerk and behind the tops of the large front-pipes. Such an organ was known as Oberwerk. Sometimes, in the 18th century, its pipes were boxed in and it became an Echo organ. When only three manuals were provided, there were no hard and fast rules concerning which should come first, the Brustwerk or the Oberwerk. Indeed, in the 18th century, an Oberwerk was sometimes provided instead of a proper Rückpositiv. Moreover, in and after the middle of the 18th century, the whole of the divisions of the organ were frequently put into one case. As Schweitzer notes, this was a retrograde step and took from the organ an important means of permitting the contrapuntal lines of organ-music to separate themselves just sufficiently in the perception of the listener. Thus were the seeds sown of a movement which culminated during the last hundred years, and led to the haphazard packing of organs into various spare corners, and their parts into any small empty spaces which gave a convenient hiding-place for them. This ushered in the final decadence of the romantic instrument! To-day in many parts of the world, notably in the United States of America and in the Germanic and Norse states of Europe, there is a healthy tendency to return to sound structural and dispositional designs in organ-building.

The specifications of six organs on which Bach played now follow:

Bonifaciuskirche, Arnstadt in Thuringia
built in 1703 by Johann Friedrich Wender

[Bach was appointed organist on July 13th, 1703, at the age of eighteen. He played on Sundays from 8 a.m. to 10 a.m., on Thursdays from 7 a.m. to 9 a.m. and usually at services on Mondays].

OBERWERK (lower keyboard)		Ft.	BRUST POSITIV (upper keyboard)		Ft.	PEDAL		Ft.
1. Prinzipal	..	8				1. Sub-bass ..	..	16
2. Quintaton ..	..	16	1. Prinzipal ..	..	4	2. Prinzipalbass	..	8
3. Viola da gamba	..	8	2. Gedackt ..	..	8	3. Flötenbass	..	4
4. Gedackt ..	..	8	3. Spitzflöte ..	..	4	4. Posaune ..	..	16
5. Gemshorn	..	8	4. Nachthorn	..	4	5. Cornet bass	..	2
6. Quinte	6 (5½)		5. Quinte ..	3 (2⅔)				
7. Octava	..	4	6. Sesquialtera	II rks.		**ACCESSORIES**		
8. Cymbel ..	III rks.		7. Mixtur ..	IV rks.		Manual koppel		
9. Mixtur ..	IV rks.		8. Octave ..	..	2	Pedalkoppel zum Oberwerk		
10. Trompete ..	..	8				Tremulant in Oberwerk		
						Glocken-Accord (Cymbel-Stern)		

In this small organ [of which nine stops still remain in the present enlarged instrument], the first manual controlled the Oberwerk which was above the Brustwerk. Neither by its size nor its composition of stops was it considered adequate to be called Hauptwerk.

Jakobikirche, Hamburg

Built by Arp Schnitger in 1688-1692, incorporating some materials of a former organ by Scherer. [Bach applied for the post here, but the coveted position went to J. J. Heitmann who was able to pay a premium for it. " He could prelude better with thalers than with fingers," says Albert Schweitzer. The organ, but not the case, was saved throughout the 1939-1945 war and the instrument and church are now restored. The organ inspired H. H. Jahn, Albert Schweitzer and later Karl Straube, during the " new organ movement " of later years, when the errors of romanticism were swept away. Thus, it has a double interest and importance in the study of Bach's music].

HAUPTWERK

		Ft.
Prinzipal	.. ..	16
Quintaton	.. ..	16
Oktave ..	.. ..	8
Spitzflöte	.. ..	8
Gedackt	.. ..	4
Rohrflöte	.. ..	4
Superoktave	.. ..	2
Flachflöte	.. ..	2
Rauschpfeife	..	III rks.
Mixtur ..	VI-VIII rks.	
Trompete	.. ..	16

OBERWERK

		Ft.
Prinzipal	.. ..	8
Holzflöte	.. ..	8
Rohrflöte	.. ..	8
Oktave ..	.. ..	4
Spitzflöte	.. ..	4
Nasat ..	..	3 (2⅔)
Oktave ..	.. ..	2
Gemshorn	.. ..	2
Scharff ..	..	IV-VI rks.
Zimbel ..	..	III rks.

		Ft.
Trompete	.. ..	8
Vox Humana ..	..	8
Trompete	.. ..	4

Koppel Oberwerk/
  Hauptwerk
Koppel Rückpositiv/Pedal
Tremulant für Oberwerk

RÜCKPOSITIV

		Ft.
Prinzipal	.. ..	8
Gedackt	.. ..	8
Quintaton	.. ..	8
Oktave ..	.. ..	4
Blockflöte	.. ..	4
Nasat ..	..	3 (2⅔)
Oktave ..	.. ..	2
Sifflöte ..	..	1½ (1⅓)
Sesquialtera	..	II rks.
Scharff ..	..	IV-VI rks.
Dulzian..	.. ..	16
Bärpfeife	.. ..	8
Schalmei	.. ..	4

BRUSTWERK

		Ft.
Holzprinzipal ..	..	8
Oktave ..	.. ..	4
Hohlflöte	.. ..	4
Waldflöte	.. ..	2
Sesquialtera	..	II rks.
Scharff ..	..	IV-VI rks.
Dulzian..	.. ..	8
Trechterregal ..	..	8

PEDAL

		Ft.
Prinzipal	.. ..	32
Oktave ..	.. ..	16
Sub-bass	.. ..	16
Oktave ..	.. ..	8
Oktave ..	.. ..	4
Nachthorn	.. ..	2
Mixtur ..	VI-VIII rks.	
Rauschpfeife	..	III rks.
Posaune	.. ..	32
Posaune	.. ..	16
Dulzian..	.. ..	16
Trompete	.. ..	8
Trompete	.. ..	4
Kornett..	.. ..	2

Marienkirche, Lübeck

(1) *The Totentanzorgel (The Organ in the Chapel of the Dance of Death)*

HAUPTWERK (1475-77)

			Ft.
1. Quintade	..	..	16
2. Principal (front Pipes)		..	8
3. Spitzflöte	..	..	8
4. Oktave	..	..	4
5. Nasat	..	..	2⅔
6. Rauschpfeife		rks.	2
7. Mixtur	..	rks.	8-10
8. Trompete	..	..	8

BRUSTWERK (1621-1622)

			Ft.
1. Gedackt	..	..	8
2. Quintade	..	..	4
3. Hohlflöte	..	..	2
4. Quintflöte	..	..	1½
5. Scharff	..	rks.	4
6. Krummhorn	..	..	8
7. Schalmei	..	..	4

TREMULANT

Coupler Rück-positiv to Hauptwerk

RÜCK-POSITIV (c. 1550)

			Ft.
1. Principal (front Pipes)	..		8
2. Rohrflöte	..	..	8
3. Quintade	..	..	8
4. Oktave	..	..	4
5. Rohrflöte	..	..	4
6. Sesquialtera..	..	rks.	2
7. Sifflöte	..	..	1½
8. Scharff	..	.. rks.	6-8
9. Dulcian	..	..	16
10. Trechterregal	..	..	8

PEDAL (1475-77, 1621-22)

				Ft.
1. Principal (front Pipes)		..		16
2. Sub-bass	..	..	..	16
3. Oktave	..	..		8
4. Gedackt	..	..		8
5. Oktave	..	..		4
6. Quintade	..	..		4
7. Oktave	..	..		2
8. Nachthorn..	..			1
9. Zimbel	..	..	rks.	2
10. Mixtur	..	..	rks.	4
11. Posaune	..	..		16
12. Dulcian	..	..		16
13. Trompete	..	..		8
14. Schalmei	..	..		4
15. Cornett	..	..		2

(2) *The large Organ*

HAUPTWERK

			Ft.
1. Principal	..	..	16
2. Quintadena		..	16
3. Octava	..	..	8
4. Spitzflöte	..	..	8
5. Octava	..	..	4
6. Hohlflöte	..	..	4
7. Nasat	..	3 (2⅔)	
8. Rauschpfeiffe	.. rks.		4
9. Scharff	..	rks.	4
10. Mixtura	..	rks.	15
11. Trommete	..	..	16
12. Trommete	..	..	8
13. Zinck	..	..	8

BRUSTWERK

			Ft.
1. Principal	..	..	8
2. Gedackt	..	..	8
3. Octava	..	..	4
4. Hohlflöte	..	..	4
5. Sesquialtera..	..	rks.	2
6. Feld-pfeiffe ..	..	..	2
7. Gemshorn ..	..	..	2
8. Sifflet	..	(1⅓')	1½
9. Mixtura	..	rks.	8
10. Cimbel	..	rks.	3
11. Krumhorn ..	..	..	8
12. Regal	..	..	8

RÜCK-POSITIV

			Ft.
1. Principal	..	..	8
2. Bordun	..	..	16
3. Blockflöte	..	..	8
4. Sesquialtera..	..	rks.	2
5. Hohlflöte	..	..	8
6. Quintadena	..	..	8
7. Octava	..	..	4
8. Spiel-flöte	..	..	2
9. Mixtura	..	rks.	5
10. Dulzian	..	..	16
11. Baarpfeiffe ..	..	..	8
12. Trichter-Regal	..	..	8
13. Vox Humana	..	..	8
14. Scharff	..	rks.	4-5

PEDAL

			Ft.
1. Principal	..	..	32
2. Sub-bass	..	..	16
3. Octava	..	..	8
4. Bauerflöte	..	..	2
5. Mixtura	..	rks.	6
6. Gross-Posaune	..	..	24
7. Posaune	..	..	16
8. Trommete	..	..	8
9. Principal	..	..	16
10. Gedackt	..	..	8
11. Octava	..	..	4
12. Nachthorn ..	..	..	2
13. Dulzian	..	..	16
14. Krumhorn ..	..	..	8
15. Cornet	..	..	2

Cimbelstern
16 Bellows
2 Drums
Inter-manual Couplers
2 Tremulants (one to Pedal)
Ventils to each Section

In October, 1705, Bach asked for four weeks of absence in order to go to Lübeck to hear the Abendmusik of Dietrich Buxtehude. He made the long journeys of about 250 miles each way on foot, and actually stayed away for four months.

The organ, by various builders at different times, had an enormous West-end case with 32 ft. pipes in the front. The organs of the Church were destroyed in an air-raid on Palm Sunday night, 1942, but the contents of the large organ had been completely replaced by a new instrument, made by J. F. Schulze, in the middle of the nineteenth century.

Until its destruction in 1942, the Totentanz organ was probably the oldest instrument in Germany whose history could be traced. It stood at the entrance to a chapel, which was decorated with paintings of the Dance of Death, commemorating a plague which struck the city in the fourteenth century. The " Totentanz-orgel " was first built in 1492. It was moved in 1547-48 to the chapel, where it stood for nearly four hundred years. The organ case was lavishly gilded over a blue ground.

Schlosskirche, Weimar

HAUPTWERK (upper keyboard)		Ft.	POSITIV (lower keyboard)		Ft.
1. Quintaton	..	16	1. Prinzipal	..	8
2. Prinzipal	..	8	2. Viola di gamba	..	8
3. Gemshorn	..	8	3. Gedackt	..	8
4. Gedackt	..	8	4. Kleingedackt	..	4
5. Octave	..	4	5. Octave	..	4
6. Quintaton	..	4	6. Waldflöte	..	2
7. Mixtur	..	VI rks.	7. Sesquialtera..	II rks.	
8. Cymbel	..	III rks.	8. Trompeta	..	8
9. Glockenspiel	..				

PEDAL		Ft.
1. Gros untersatz	..	32
2. Sub-bass	..	16
3. Violon bass	..	16
4. Prinzipal bass	..	8
5. Posaune bass	..	16
6. Trompeten ..	..	8
7. Cornetten bass	..	4

1. Tremulant to Hauptwerk
2. Tremulant to Unterwerk (Positiv)
3. Pedalkoppel zum Hauptwerk
4. Coppelung der Manual Claviere
5. Cymbel Stern

Bach played the organ in the Schlosskirche (Castle Church), Weimar, from 1708 to 1717, which was a most fertile period for his organ compositions. The Castle Church, originally St. Martin's Church, was burnt down in 1618 and a new building to replace it was constructed for Duke Wilhelm IV in 1658. The new chapel was very high in comparison with its length and breadth. It was surrounded by three galleries and the organ was above the altar at the top of the building. The chapel was known as " der Weg zur Himmelsburg," and it was decorated with a blue sky and white cherubim ascending towards the celestial organ. It is not unlikely that the situation of the organ and the visual biblical symbolism of the chapel were reflected in the organ works of the Weimar period. The organ was built by Ludwig Compenius in 1657, and was later rebuilt by Weishaupt and Trebs. In 1715, the latter added to the organ a new " Nürnberg Glockenspiel." The castle and chapel were burnt down in 1774 in an enormous conflagration. It is interesting to note that the organ in the Castle Church had the " kornett-tone " or highest Chorton, which gave it a pitch a minor third above " chamber-tone".

Frauenkirche, Dresden

The organ, specified below, is typical of a different school of organ-building from that of the North European Arp Schnitger. The organ in the Frauenkirche in Dresden was one of the master works of Gottfried Silbermann. It was built in 1736, approved by Friedemann Bach, and played in a recital by Johann Sebastian Bach on December 1st of the same year. The organ was destroyed with the church in the second World War.

HAUPTWERK	Ft.	BRUSTWERK	
Prinzipal	16	Gedackt ..	8
Oktave ..	8	Prinzipal	4
Gambe ..	8	Rohrflöte	4
Rohrflöte	8	Nasat ..	3 (2⅔)
Oktave ..	4	Oktave ..	2
Spitzflöte	4	Gemshorn	2
Quinte ..	3 (2⅔)	Quinte ..	1½ (1⅓)
Oktave ..	2	Sifflöte ..	1
Terz ..	1³/₅	Mixtur ..	III rks.
Kornett ..	IV rks.	Schalmei ..	8
Mixtur ..	IV rks.		
Cymbel ..	III rks.		
Fagott ..	16		
Trompete	8		

OBERWERK	Ft.	PEDAL	
Quintatön	16		Ft.
Prinzipal	8	Untersatz ..	32
Gedackt ..	8	Prinzipal bass ..	16
Quintaton	8	Posaunenbass ..	16
Oktave ..	4	Oktavbass	8
Rohrflöte	4	Trompetbass ..	8
Nasat ..	3 (2⅔)	Oktavbass	4
Oktave ..	2	Claironbass	4
Terz ..	1³/₅	Mixturenbass ..	VI rks.
Mixtur ..	IV rks.		
Vox humana			
Klarinette	8		

THE NATURE OF THE STOPS IN THE ORGANS PLAYED BY BACH

ALTHOUGH it is impossible to describe tone-quality precisely in words, some remarks concerning the nature of the stops in the organs which Bach played are necessary, if only to distinguish them from the similarly-named registers of 19th and 20th century organs. During the life-time of Bach the German organ was an instrument of transition. Before the Thirty Years' War (1618-1648) the early Baroque instruments commanded a wealth of tonalities which was not to be heard again until recent times, and then only rarely. The late 16th and early 17th centuries saw the production of an enormous variety of organ-pipes, particularly in the shapes of the flue-pipes and the tubes or resonators of the reeds. After the Thirty Years' War, recovery was slow until the end of the 17th century, and then there was a tendency to reduce the resources of the organ. In spite of the perfection to which Gottfried Silbermann brought his flue choruses, and the wonder of the blend of tone in his organs, his work contained the seeds of unfortunate tendencies. For instance, his pedal organs rarely showed the versatility which was to be found in Schnitger's organs. Again, not infrequently he overlooked the vertical disposition of the sections of the organ, so essential a part of the conception of the Baroque instrument, and he packed away the whole organ in a single case. To enter any criticism against the great master Silbermann may seem to be churlish and unfair; but it seems probable that the Schnitger organs, if properly understood, will yield a better clue to the organ music of Bach and his immediate predecessors.

The Principal Chorus

The pitch of the Principal (unison open flue stop) differed on each manual and pedal. We might find that of the pedal of a large organ as 32 ft., of the Hauptwerk 16 ft., the Rückpositiv 8 ft., the Brustwerk or Oberwerk 4 ft., or on smaller organs, the Principal pitch of the Pedal 16 feet, that of the Hauptwerk 8 ft. and the Rückpositiv 4 ft. The Principal choruses of the 17th and early 18th centuries bore little relationship to a modern Diapason Chorus. The Principal stops were called the " narrow-scaled " or " male " stops, and the choruses contained only octave- and fifth-sounding ranks. The impression to the ear was that of a rich, mezzoforte tone which would become bright and brilliant when the mixtures were added. In constrast to the principal choruses on each manual there were sets, and sometimes families of " wide scaled " or " female " stops, such as flutes, quintatöns, tierces, cornets.

In the 19th century, there was a tendency to make the various ranks of a principal chorus of the same scale. In the 16th, 17th and usually in the 18th centuries, organ-builders generally made their organs in the buildings in which they were to speak. The scalings of the pipes were empirical and much time was spent in making final adjustments.[1] A good principal chorus was easy to listen to – it was bright, cheerful, transparent, full and gentle at the same time, and " contrapuntal " in the sense that all the parts of a fugue could be heard. No greater contrast to this can be imagined than the noisy, opaque, diapason " choruses," founded on leathered, unison-diapasons, and topped with compound stops containing tierces, which were *le dernier cri* in some English Cathedrals of the 20th century. Although the principal stops of the 16th, 17th and early 18th century organs spoke naturally and quickly, the initiation

---

[1] Although the traffic outside churches must have been comparatively light in those days, organ-builders often insisted that the churches and surrounding roads should be closed for some months, during which time the final tonal adjustments were made.

characteristic of their tone, known as a " chiff," was not pronounced in this type of tone; nor was any attempt made to exaggerate it. It was more prominent in the flute and other wide-scaled stops.

The 'Wide-scaled' Stops

Omitting, for the present, stops of the gamba class (which in the 17th and 18th centuries had a broad, non-imitative tone hardly recognisable as being of string quality), we may set out the stops of a Hauptwerk manual as follows:

GROUP I *" principal, male or narrow-scale "*	Ft.	GROUP II *" female or wide-scale "*	Ft.
Prinzipal	8	Quintadena	16
Oktave	4	Rohrflöte	8
Quinte	3 (2⅔)	Spitzflöte	4
Oktav	2	Nasat	3 (2⅔)
Mixtur	VIII rks.	Gemshorn	2
Trompete	16	Sesquialtera	II rks.
		Baarpfeife 8 (a type of regal with squat, wide tubes), or Vox Humana	

The female or wide-scaled stops were of highly individual tone-quality, and although the tone was sometimes duller than that of the principal-scaled stops it was never thick and muddy. Moreover, most, if not all, of these stops were of metal construction. The Quintadena family of stops produced tone qualities in which the twelfth was as prominent as the ground tone – and sometimes more so. The rohrflöte was of wide, cylindrical, metal construction: each pipe was surmounted with a metal canister with a hole to which was soldered a vertical tube. The tone quality, which is pleasing and interesting, cannot be imitated by pipes of ordinary gedact type. The gemshorn and spitzflöte pipes tapered inwards towards the tops of their open metal pipes. This produced a pleasing piquancy, and a slight reediness in the tone because of the presence of the 17th and higher harmonics. Another important stop of peculiar construction was the koppelflöte, which was sometimes called spillflöte or spindle-flute. In the pipes of such stops a cylindrical body was surmounted by an inverted cone so that the pipe looked, at first sight, as though it had feet at both ends. Again, it had a beautiful and characteristic tonality. It was called koppelflöte[1] because it could function as a medium for the mixing of other tones, and as the unison above which tonal-pyramids of stops of higher pitch could be erected. The mutation ranks of duller tone, which could be mixed together to make new tonal qualities, in a manner characteristic of the organ, were classed with the wide-scaled stops. The tierce, a 17th and " third-sounding " stop, gave

---

[1] This is the same type of stop as copel, coppel, copula which was and is found on the Austrian organs played by Mozart.

a reedy, sometimes growling tone quality to other stops to which it was added. The sesquialtera, the chief and sometimes sole ingredients of which were the piquant twelfth and the reedy tierce, was useful in solo combinations, because of the powerful colour which it gave them. The cornet, which was composed of ranks of large-scale pipes, in harmonic order, may be regarded as a tonal completion of the sesquialtera. The pipes were made of a metal containing a high proportion of lead; and, although the individual ranks of the cornet might seem to be dull, their combination gave a tone which possessed a strong reed-like quality. Thus, the wide-scaled stops, used alone or in combination at different pitches, would produce a palette which would yield an almost inexhaustible variety of tone-colours. For the playing of the melodies of chorales these natural organ-tones were of far more interest and value than the orchestral " imitations " to be found in the solo organs of the late 19th and early 20th centuries, beautiful though some of these are.

Since Bach cast aside the traditional rules of registration and was completely pragmatic in his approach to the problems of organ tone-colour, it is imagined that he did not separate the tones of the principal stops and the wide scale stops when he found that the result was aurally pleasing. It is outside the scope of this book to deal in detail with the enormous number of different types of tone to be found in the 17th century organ in Europe.

The reader is invited to consult the works listed in the bibliography at the end of this volume.

Reed Tone

" *The greatest organist and expert on organs in Germany, and perhaps in Europe, the late Kapellmeister Bach, was a friend of the reeds; he for one must have known what could be played on them, and how. Is the convenience of some organists and organ-builders really reason enough to scorn such stops, to call them names, and to eliminate them?*

" *In the organ of St. Catherine's Church in Hamburg there are sixteen reeds. The late Kapellmeister, Mr. J. S. Bach, in Leipzig, who once made himself heard for two full hours on this instrument, which he called excellent in all its parts, could not praise the beauty and variety of tone of these reeds highly enough. It is known, too, that the former organist of this church, Mr. Johann Adam Reinken, always kept them in the best tune.*

" *The late Kapellmeister Bach in Leipzig gave assurance that the 32 ft. Principal and the pedal Trombone (32 ft.) in the organ at St.*

Catherine's Church in Hamburg spoke evenly and quite audibly down to the lowest C. But he also used to say that this principal was the only one as good as that, of such size, that he had heard."[1]

We do not need to seek far in order to find the reason for the unpopularity of the reeds with many organists. Werckmeister, writing when Bach was young, says

> " *Schnarrwerke is the work of fools,*
> *but when it is pure and good,*
> *it rejoices heart and mind.*"[2]

A considerable variety of reed-work is illustrated and described in Praetorius's Syntagma (Organographia, Volume 2, 1619). The Schnarrwerke mentioned above refers to the gruff-toned regals of which there were many patterns. These had small resonators of different shapes. Thus there were trichter (trechter), apfel, knop regals etc., with funnel, apple and " head "-shaped tubes respectively. Vox humanas were of this class and it was imagined that male and female voices could be imitated by using different types of reed tubes. Such small reed-pipes soon got out of tune and regulation. And this made them intolerable unless they received attention from a skilful organist or organ-builder.

When they were in proper order such reeds had highly coloured, distinctive tones. Their speech commenced with a characteristic sound; they were penetrating in tone, but of no great power. In fact, in the Baroque organ there was comparatively little difference in power between one rank of pipes and another. Some of the higher-pitched pedal reeds, such as zink and schalmei, which had some slight resemblance in tone to the instruments of those names respectively, had a not unpleasant snarling and penetrating tone which gave great colour and independence to the pedal melody. Reeds of regal type were often found in the Brustwerk section. Here they could easily be reached by the organist who could tune and adjust them before playing them. The ability to do this was a part of the necessary skill of the organist.

The regal type of reed tended to fall into disfavour in the second half of the 18th century, especially in the middle of Germany and the Southern States. Compound flue stops were supplied in the place of these reeds of uncertain behaviour, but they were not adequate substitutes for reed tone which was in tune and well-regulated. There were also reeds which had long, conical tubes, and these had a moderately-loud, trumpet tone. Even so, when

---

[1] J. F. Agricola: " Treatise on the Organ and Other Instruments " contained in Adlung's " Musica Mechanica Organoedi."

[2] " Orgelprobe " [Organ proving and testing] — a work intended to help organists and church authorities to judge organs and organ-builders.

they were added to a principal chorus they did not engulf it, but gave it a fine rich tone.

It will have been observed already that the trompete was classed with the narrow-scaled stops: its tone was thin, penetrating and moderate in power.

Bach's Organ Playing

Most of the accounts of Bach's organ-playing are imaginative and give little real technical information, but the following account in a letter written by C. P. E. Bach to Forkel (Johann Sebastian's biographer) is significant:

" *No-one has ever tried out organs so severely and yet at the same time so honestly as he. He understood the whole building of organs in the highest degree. When an organ-builder had worked conscientiously and incurred losses by his work, he would persuade the employers to make amends. No-one understood registration as well as he. Organ-builders were terrified when he sat down to play their organs and drew the stops in his own manner, for they thought that the effect would not be as good as he was planning it; then they heard an effect that astounded them.*" [*A marginal note goes on to add " These Sciences perished with him.*"]   " *The first thing he would do in trying an organ was this. He would say, in jest, 'Above all, I must know whether the organ has good lungs,' and, to find out, he would draw out every speaking stop, and play in the fullest and richest possible texture. At this the organ-builder would often grow quite pale with fright.*"

Thus, there is evidence to show that Bach approached the problems of registration with a completely open mind. Before his day there were strict rules concerning registration and two, in particular, are interesting:

(a) Only one unison stop must be used at a time on any one division of the organ.

(b) Stops of Principal (small-scale or male) type must not be mixed with those of wide-scale (female) type.

Bach's prescience, judgement and aural acuity were such that he could imagine what type of composite tone would result by blending a number of individual tone colours. The marginal note quoted above which says " These Sciences (i.e. of registration) perished with him," is doubtless true, but any organist with patience and perception could find suitable mélanges of stops by experimentation with individual ranks; indeed, all thoughtful organists should spend considerable time doing this. It is recorded that Felix Mendelssohn experimented for hours with large organs in Frankfurt at a time when he was composing his Sonatas and practising the organ works of J. S. Bach.

THE USE OF THE DIVISIONS OF THE ORGAN
Space Placement: The Werk-Principle

C. P. E. BACH, writing about his father to Forkel, says, " He made good use of any space. He grasped at the first glance the sound properties of any space."

The spatial use of the various divisions of the organ was a characteristic of the works of the Northern organists. For instance, in the preludes and fugues of Buxtehude, Reinken and other Northern organists, the numerous short sections could only be realised by using Hauptwerk, Brustwerk, Rückpositiv or Oberwerk and pedal according to the " werk-principle." Without the aid of an assistant stop-changing was not easy, and was often impossible during the playing of a movement. Exaggerated dynamic contrasts were not required, and each part of the organ made its impression because of its timbre and position. The swell pedal, invented in Iberia and used in England during the earlier lifetime of Bach, was not used in the German organ. Echo effects were popular, and sometimes the pipes of the Oberwerk section, high above the Hauptwerk, were screened or boxed-up to some extent in order that such effects could be produced. In the Dorian Toccata (BWV 538) Bach specifies Rückpositif and Oberwerk, and in the arrangements, as Organ Concerti, from Vivaldi's works, he specifies Rückpositif, Oberwerk and Brustwerk. Thus, changes of tone-quality, pitch, dynamics and source of tone were possible at the finger-tips of the organist. Rapid changes of manual are marked in the chorale-prelude *Christ lag in Todesbanden*/ Christ lay in the bonds of death (BWV 625), and are necessary for the effective playing of the Fugue in G (à la Gigue, BWV 577),[1] which probably was conceived originally for a two-manual and pedal clavichord or harpsichord.

Cantus firmus Pedal

Thus, many of Bach's organ compositions can only be interpreted fully when the spatial relationships of each section of the organ are considered with reference to the music, e.g. the Prelude and Fugue in Eb (BWV 552). The principal chorus of the Hauptwerk is contrasted with the flue-work of the Positiv. The Hauptwerk paints on a large canvas with its depth, height and breadth in its physical size and, by analogy, in its sound. The Positiv, which probably sounds almost as loud as the Hauptwerk, is nearer to the hearer and less extensive, both physically and as a source of sound.

---

[1] It is necessary to state that some doubts have been cast on the authenticity of this as a composition by J. S. Bach.

Consider also the Prelude and Fugue in C Minor (BWV 546); the Toccata and Fugue in D minor (BWV 565); the Prelude and Fugue in D (BWV 532) and generally the great Preludes and Fugues, Toccatas and Fantasias. Here are massive effects for Hauptwerk and pedal in the main case, episodes for the bright tone of the Rückpositiv and contrasting or echo effects between the Brustwerk (which was below the Hauptwerk) and the Oberwerk (above the Hauptwerk).

The use of the parts of the organ in the Chorale Preludes is even more subtle. Against the large back-cloth of a quiet Hauptwerk and pedal, used as an accompaniment, the chorale-melody is projected from the Rückpositiv or other small section. The propinquity of the Positiv tone, heard by those sitting in the nave, at no great distance from the instrument, would add to the psychological impact of the chorale-tune. Many of the more complex ornaments and elaborate decorations of the tune, as in *Wenn wir in höchsten Nöten sein* / When we are in deepest need (BWV 641), and *O Mensch, bewein* / Mankind bewail thine awful sin (BWV 622) would be feasible on the Positiv or Brustwerk, with their light touch, of many larger organs. It does not seem to be fanciful to suggest that the tones of the Oberwerk, coming from the top of the organ case, would be appropriate for use in such works as *Vom Himmel hoch* / From heaven above (BWV 606) and *Vom Himmel kam der Engel Schaar* / From Heaven came the angel host (BWV 607). The organ in the chapel at Weimar which was placed " celestially " seems to suggest some of the spatial effects for the playing of the Chorale Preludes. The design and decoration of the chapel, which were intended to represent the journey from earth to heaven, may not have been without their effects on the thoughts of the composer, at a period in his life most fertile in organ composition.

It should be mentioned that the Hauptwerk principal of the seventeenth and eighteenth-century organ was not too loud to accompany mf solos on the Positiv. Late in the eighteenth century, Dom Bédos suggested that the 4 ft. rank should be added to the montre (front pipes) 8 ft. if the latter was too soft for use as an accompaniment!

All the Concerti after Vivaldi (BWV 592-5) contain interesting use of Oberwerk and Rückpositiv with occasional use of Organo pleno; and the use of forte and piano in contrast is indicated in the Partitas, *Christ der du bist der helle Tag* / Christ, Thou art the bright day (BWV 766); *O Gott, du frommer Gott* / O God, Thou faithful God (BWV 767); *Ach, was ist doch unser Leben* / Alas, what is this life of ours? (BWV 743).

PRO ORGANO PLENO

THIS marking is given for: Prelude and Fugue in Eb (BWV 552); Prelude and Fugue in B minor (BWV 544) and for other great Preludes and Fugues and Toccatas. The Chorale Prelude *Wir glauben all' an einen Gott, Schöpfer* / We all believe in God, Creator (BWV 680), sometimes called " The Giant's Fugue "; *Komm', Gott Schöpfer, Heiliger Geist* / Come, God Creator, Holy Spirit (BWV 667); Fantasia on *Komm' Heil'ger Geist, Herre Gott* / Come, Lord God, the Holy Spirit (BWV 651); *Nun komm', der Heiden Heiland* / Come, Thou Saviour of the Gentiles (BWV 661); the Prelude and Fugue in C major (BWV 566) (given in E in some copies); the Allabreve in D (BWV 589); the Praeludium in C (BWV 943); the last variation in the Partita *Sei gegrüsset Jesu* / Be greeted, gracious Jesus (BWV 768) and in a passage in the first movement of the second of the arrangements from Vivaldi's Violin Concerti (BWV 593). It is also appropriate for the Toccatas and Fugues of the Northern masters, and for some of the works of Sweelinck, Gabrieli, Merulo and Frescobaldi.

Organo Pleno does not mean " full organ " in the sense that all the stops are drawn, but sometimes it refers to the use of the resources of a large and well-appointed organ, by seventeenth century standards.

In general *Organo Pleno* is the equivalent of the French *plein jeu*, the tonal ingredients of which are given by Dom Bédos in his great volumes on organ-building. The term can be traced back to the " organo pieno " of the sixteenth and seventeenth century Italian organs. The principal-scaled full flue-work on the manuals is drawn and care is taken not to sully its mezzoforte transparency with thick-toned flutes or cornets (but in the French organ the fourniture and cymbales are allowed). The use of the tierce and other third-sounding ranks is not permitted. To the full small-scaled pedal-fluework the reeds of thin but penetrating trumpet tone are added. Tonal clarity on both manuals and pedals is the keynote here. All the contrapuntal lines must be heard, and the pedal must stand out slightly, so that it is not overborne by the manual tones, and does not need reinforcement by coupling to the manuals.[1] The power of the Rückpositiv flue-work is comparable in power with that of the Hauptwerk and certainly not less than half of it. Moreover, the pipes of the Rückpositiv are nearer to the listener, at

---

[1] The pedal division of the romantic organ was not only indefinite in tonality, but it was emaciated in bulk. Even to provide a suitable bass it had to be coupled to the manuals. Moreover, it lacked precise disposition in space with respect to the manual divisions. It is not surprising that there were overlappings which obscured part-writing when the coupler Great to Pedal perforce had to become so important.

a lower level in the church and sufficiently separated in space from those of the Hauptwerk to give an effect of gentle contrast. The tone of the *Organo Pleno* is full, bright and, in large organs, weighty and dignified, but it is satisfying and does not soon weary the ear.

On the other hand, it is possible that the words *Pro Organo Pleno* sometimes referred to louder, extended pieces suitable for postludes.

DOPPIO PEDALE

BACH and his predecessors often call for the use of double-pedalling. With many organs of the last hundred years this useful device of *Doppio Pedale* produces thick, turgid and unsatisfactory effects, even if the 16 feet stops are not used. The tone of the old German pedal organ was just as clear and definite as that of the Hauptwerk. Moreover, the idea that 16 ft. was the normal pitch of the pedal organ had to be eschewed. Many of the 16th century organs, particularly in North Europe and France, contained 16 ft. stops on the manuals, but only 8 ft. and 4 ft. flue and reed stops on the pedals. If, in contrapuntal compositions, any melodic line could be considered as more important than any other, that line could be written in any of the staves and be played with the necessary slight prominence by right hand, left hand or feet alike.

The homophonic organ and the homophonic organ-works of later years interacted on one another to the advantage of neither. The organ of Bach was essentially contrapuntal.

Examples of *Doppio Pedale* which require transparent, bright and precise tone in J. S. Bach's works will be found in: Prelude in D major (BWV 532); *Aus tiefer Noth* / In deepest need (BWV 686); *An Wasserflüssen Babylon* / By the Waters of Babylon (BWV 653b); *Wir glauben all' an einen Gott Vater* / We all believe in God, the Father (BWV 740).

It is interesting to note that the baroque pedal organs, particularly in North Germany, commanded more independent stops than the chief manual of the organ.

Some of the Schübler Chorale Preludes have registration markings. Two, *Kommst du nun, Jesu* / Come Thou now, Jesu (BWV 650) and *Wer nur den lieben Gott lässt walten* / If thou wilt but accept God's guidance (BWV 647) are both marked " ped. 4 fuss," which was almost certainly a 4 ft. pedal reed. The Chorale Prelude *Wo soll ich fliehen hin* / Whither shall I flee? (BWV 646) is marked " 1 clav. 8 fuss, 2 clav. 16 fuss, ped. 4 fuss". This is interesting as an example of the extent of the freedom of the manuals and pedals with regard to pitch. This was no original scheme of Bach's, but was in the style of the earlier North German, Dutch and French masters, in which an incisive, rather than loud pedal reed, sustained the *cantus firmus* or chorale-melody, with canonic working between the manual parts. The three canonic preludes are marked as follows:

a) *Gottes Sohn ist kommen* / The Son of God is come (BWV 600). Prinzipal 8 fuss (manual) pedal Trompete 8 fuss.

b) The Christmas hymn *In dulci jubilo* (BWV 608) has pedal 8 ft. reed indicated, but if the pedal-board does not go up to G, then a 4 ft. reed must be used on the pedal and the part played an octave lower. On many 19th and 20th century organs it is difficult or impossible to find the correct tone at this pitch, even by coupling a manual to the pedal.

c) *O Lamm Gottes, unschuldig* / O guiltless Lamb of God (BWV 618) the pedal is also marked 8 ft. reed, and here again great care must be taken to secure the correct phrasing.

[Examples of other Chorale Preludes where the chorale melody should be given to an independent pedal of distinctive tone are *Valet will ich dir geben* / I bid thee now farewell (BWV 735); *Nun freut euch* / Be joyful now (BWV 734); *Christ, unser Herr, zum Jordan kam* / Christ our Lord to Jordan came (BWV 684)].

The Adagio of the Toccata, Adagio and Fugue appears to be an example of a solo combination of stops being used to play full harmonies at the end of the movement.

As has been indicated before, much concerning Bach's use of the stops of the organ is a matter of conjecture. It does not seem likely that there would be much possibility of changing stops during a fugal movement. It is true, of course, that assistants could be used for this purpose. Also, in Bach's time, ventil pedals appeared on a few organs, and these would admit or cut off the wind from whole chests at a time, and could be used for adding or subtracting blocks of stops; often there was an inter-manual coupler. This was brought into operation by pulling one manual forward over the other, a distance of a few inches, by means of knobs on each side of the manual. With all these, however, there can be no doubt that Bach would avoid the pitfall, which has trapped so many organists of more recent times, of destroying the structure inherent in a fugue by overlaying it with violent changes of registration.

THE YOUNG BACH'S EXPERT ORGAN ADVICE

An interesting light on Bach's ideas concerning the tonal equipment of an organ, when he was still in his " early twenties," is found in his expert advice concerning an organ which he was to play, as organist, in Mühlhausen. Some of his proposals have an almost romantic flavour, and it may be that as he grew older he became more austere in his use of organ tone.

Bach's Memorandum concerning the Organ at St. Blasiuskirche at Mühlhausen

[Bach was twenty-two years old at the time and had recently become organist of the church].

" 1. The lack of wind must be made up by the addition of three good new bellows to take care of the Oberwerck, the Rückpositiv and the new Brustwerck.

2. The four old bellows now present must be adapted, with stronger wind pressure, to the new 32-foot Sub-bass and the other bass stops.

3. The old wind chests must all be taken out and freshly supplied with such wind conduction that one stop alone and also the stops together can be used without alteration of the pressure, which has never been possible in the past and yet is very necessary.

4. Then follows the 32-foot Sub-Bass or so-called Untersatz of wood, which gives the whole organ the most solid foundation. This stop must now have its own wind-chest.

5. The Trombone Bass must be supplied with new and larger pipes, and the stop should be so made and arranged that it can produce a much more solid tone.

6. The new chimes desired by the parishioners to be added to the Pedal, consisting of 26 bells of 4-foot tone; which bells the parishioners will acquire at their own expense, and the organ-builder will then install them.

7. As regards the Upper Manual, instead of the Trumpet (which will be taken out) a Fagotto of 16 ft. will be installed, which is useful for all sorts of new ideas (inventiones) and sounds very well in (concerted) music.

8. Further, in place of the Gemshorn (which is likewise to be taken out) there is to be a Viol di Gamba 8 foot, which will concord admirably with the 4-foot salicional already included in the Rückpositiv. *Item*, instead of the 3-foot Quinta (which is also to be taken out).

9. A 3-foot ($2\frac{2}{3}$ foot) Nassat could be installed. The other stops now included in the Upper Manual can remain, as also the entire Rückpositiv, although all of these must be tuned in the course of the repairs.

10. Now as far as the most important matter is concerned, the new Brustwerck, the following stops could be included in it. In front, three Principals (i.e., stops of principal scale), namely:

(a) Quinta 3 foot
(b) Octava 2 foot
(c) Schalemoy (Schalmei 8 foot)
of good 14 oz. tin.[1]
(d) Mixture, three ranks.
(e) Tertia, with which, by drawing a few other stops, one can produce a fine and complete Sesquialtera.

[This stop was of $1\frac{3}{5}$ ft. pitch].

(f) Flûte douce 4 foot, and finally a
(g) Stillgedeckt 8 foot, such as accords well with (concerted) music, and made of good wood, should sound much better than a metal Gedeckt.

11. Between the manuals of this Brustwerck and Oberwerck there must be a coupler.

And finally, in addition to the complete tuning of the whole organ, the tremulant must be regulated so that it beats at the proper rate."

When we consider this, in order to obtain clues concerning Bach's registration ideas, it appears that he was seeking a variety of tone colours; in particular, he seems to have been interested in stops of the viol or gamba type. It is noteworthy that he wished that the tremulant should be put into proper order. Some writers have inferred that because the new chimes were " desired by the parishioners " they were not desired by the organist. Nevertheless, Bach was fond of bell-motives in his chorale-preludes and cantatas. The recurring pedal figure, repeated seventeen times, in the joyful chorale-prelude for the New Year, *In dir ist Freude | In Thee is joy* (BWV 615) is certainly enhanced by the addition of bell-tone to the pedals; in fact, unless the repeated theme is made bright and lively, it is difficult to avoid monotony in this work, which is intended to express optimistic high spirits.

---

[1] i.e. 14/16 of the metal (i.e. $87\frac{1}{2}\%$) is tin.

EIN' FESTE BURG IST UNSER GOTT/
A SAFE STRONGHOLD OUR GOD IS STILL (BWV 720)

BACH'S relation and friend Walther[1] brought away from the inaugural concert at Mühlhausen a copy of this Chorale Prelude which had been marked with the registration of the player. In the duo parts Bach's scheme called for Hauptwerk 16 ft. fagotto and Rückpositiv sesquialtera. It has sometimes been assumed that these stops were added to neutral flue stops. This is possible, but even as it stands this registration is in the style of the French *duo* between a fagotto on one manual and a sesquialtera or small cornet on another. Such stops were used in this way in the time of Nicolas de Grigny's *Livre d'Orgue*, which Bach copied, and were given as late as *c.* 1770 by Dom Bédos in his monumental work on organ-building.

THE TREMULANT

SINCE Bach insisted that organ-builders should make tremulants work properly (although no marking in any of his scores calls for the use of this stop), it seems probable that he did not ignore it in his playing. Organ-builders frequently provided two types of tremulant in the same organ. One worked slowly and yet vigorously and the other produced a gentle, hovering sound as its name (Schwebung) would imply. It tended to cover up irregularities in the tones of the reeds, by imposing on them its own regular vibration. It was used to imitate the slurring of the bow in string-playing. Samuel Scheidt (1587-1654) describes it as " a dignified stop and one of importance on the organ." In his " Tabulatura Nova " there is a passage intended to imitate *on other keyboard instruments* the organ tremulant: Variatio 5 of the variations on "Ach du feiner Reiter," Samuel Scheidt: Tabulatura Nova, D.D.T., p. 62. " Bicinium imitatione Tremula Organi duobis digitis in una tantum clave manu, tum dextra, tum sinistra."

Mertel, in 1666, in his *Orgelschlüssel*, said that the use of the tremulant should be confined to sad and penitential songs and during the Sanctus. At the Halberstadt Convocation, in 1693, it was

---

[1] Two Walther compositions, edited and introduced by Wm. L. Sumner: Chorale-Partita " Meinen Jesum lass' ich nicht/I will not forsake my Jesus," with the Chorale as harmonised by J. S. Bach, together with the original German and English Words of its 6 Verses. See FAMOUS ORGAN COMPOSITIONS, Vol. 12 P.E. No. 4301p. Chorale Prelude " Ein' feste Burg/A Safe Stronghold our God is still." See CHORALE PRELUDES ANCIENT AND MODERN, Vol. 1, which contains the Chorale together with settings by Praetorius, Hanff, Buxtehude, Bach, Pachelbel, Merkel, Mendelssohn, Max Reger and Richard Arnell.

decreed that the tremulant must not be used with full organ " as its beating will shake up the instrument and send it out of tune". Lebègue (1630-1702) recommended the use of the tremulant with the vox humana, as an imitation of the human voice.

THE CYMBELSTERN

THIS was a gilded, wooden star, displayed prominently in the organ-case. When the appropriate stop was drawn, the star revolved by means of a wind motor. On each point of the star were small bells or jingles. Sometimes these were not tuned, sometimes they played the notes of the scale and sometimes C's, G's, and, less frequently, E's. The device was popular at Christmas and Epiphany, and its high-speed tinkling and rustling was a not unpleasant addition to short chorale-preludes, appropriate to these seasons. The Cymbelstern is by no means obsolete and can be heard on many old and new organs in Germany today.

PHRASING AND TOUCH

Two other considerations will help to determine the choice of stops which are to be used.

When organ-stops stand on an open sound-board their power and tone quality are fixed; but skilful attention in fingering, in order to modify note-lengths and methods of tone initiation, can be made to give the aural impression of changed dynamics and even tone-quality to a certain extent. In a similar way agogic accents can be produced. Thus, with niceties of touch, mechanical action, and stops which speak with characteristic initiation qualities, much can be done to produce eloquent phrasing on unenclosed ranks of pipes. The small reeds of the old organs spoke quickly, the gambas slowly and the gedacts almost too quickly so that it was difficult to avoid overlap. Each melody had to be considered on its own merits and, according to its nature, a suitable stop or combination of stops chosen for it. The Trio Sonatas[1] (BWV 525-530): No registration markings can be expected on these, for they were originally conceived in terms of two-manual and pedal clavichord. The general principles to be observed in playing them are (1) any destructive treatment on loud combinations is out of the question. (2) The pedal should be of definite, quick-speaking tone of predominantly 8 ft. pitch. (3) The manual parts should be contrasted by using single stops of precise speech, or interesting tone-combinations containing quiet mutation stops.

---

[1] The slow movements from three Trio Sonatas have been issued together in one small volume (P.E. No. 7043): Adagio in C m. from Sonata No. 1 in Eb, Adagio e dolce in F from Sonata No. 3 in D m., Andante in B m. from Sonata No. 4 in E m.

Even if Schweitzer's theories of Bach's word-painting in his music have been criticised, there still remains a sense of appropriateness in his use of melody and accompanimental figures. For instance, his Chorale Preludes were intended to reflect the spiritual tone of the Church's Seasons and Festivals, and the registration of the organ works would be influenced accordingly.

Registration, phrasing and touch are all bound up with the acoustical properties of the church in which the organ is played. None of Bach's churches had the long periods of reverberation which are found in the Gothic Cathedrals. One of the largest was St. Thomas's Church, Leipzig, where Bach was never *officially* the organist. This had a reverberation of about 3 seconds when empty and less than half of this when full. In general, the acoustics of the churches with which Bach was associated were sufficient to " carry " the organ tone, but still not too great to obscure fairly rapid part-writing. An example of the possibility of using a moderate degree of reverberation to enhance the effect of organ-tone is found in the Prelude in C minor (BWV 546) where massive chords are contrasted with simple melodic passages of light texture.

Every type of organ-pipe has its peculiar initiation and collapse characteristics, known as transients, when it speaks. Such transients can be controlled to a certain degree, limited by the methods of voicing and by the speed at which the pallets, which admit wind to the pipes, are opened. In an organ actuated by tracker mechanism, the speech of the pipes can be modified by skilful touch on the part of the performer. The organist, who plays such an organ and is sensitive to organ-tone and the manner in which it must be elicited, learns how to meet the needs of the types of tone which he is using, together with the proper grouping of notes and the phrasing of passages. Appropriate registration, the result of careful trials, should be found for each passage which is played.

The organ can only become a poetical, eloquent instrument – a real instrument of music – if it is made to articulate. Expression is to be sought by careful attention to note grouping, note-lengths, and by fingering which will ensure suitable attack and release, rather than by use of the swell pedal. The reader is invited to study *Articulation in Organ Playing*, by Gordon Phillips (Hinrichsen No. 1001), an important work, the music text of which consists of 31 Chorale Preludes and Chorales by Bach, forming a Little Organ Book for manuals only, with a foreword by Robert Donington.

SOME ACCOUNTS OF ORGAN-REGISTRATION IN THE SEVENTEENTH AND EARLY EIGHTEENTH CENTURIES

" Use unison tone very sparingly or not at all in full combinations."
F. Niedt: Mus. Handleitung, 1721.

" Organo Pleno requires full work in the manuals without reeds; but reeds should be added to the pedals." "A good solo effect is made by adding Waldflöte 2 ft. to Gedackt 8 ft."
J. Mattheson: Der vollkommene Kapellmeister, 1739.

" Play the Cantus Firmus in the Pedal, using its 8 ft. stop and add the Scharff mixture by coupling the Pedal to the Rückpositiv."
D. Buxtehude: Te deum laudamus.

" Right hand: Principal 4 ft. and Sesquialtera in the Rückpositiv; left hand: Viola di Gamba Canon in pedal with Kornett 2 ft. (a reed)."
J. G. Walther: Plauener Orgelbuch (1708-10) –
" *Hilf, Gott, dass mir's gelinge.*"

" Fagott 16 ft., Quintadena 8 ft., Spitzflöte – a much loved combination.

Gedackt 8 ft. with Prinzipal 4 ft., Principal tone 8 ft. 4 ft. 2 ft. for festive occasions.

Gedackt 8 ft. Nasat 3 ft. Spitzflöte 2 ft.
Gedackt 8 ft. Oktave 4 ft. Spillflöte 4 ft. (or 2 ft.).
Vox humana with Gemshorn 8 ft. or Spillpfeife 4 ft.
Rohrflöte 16 ft. Prinzipal 8 ft. (for Passion hymns).
Vox humana with Principal 4 ft.
Bordun 16 ft., Vox humana 8 ft., Spillflöte 4 ft., Nasat 3 ft."
G. F. Kaufmann. Harmon. Seelenlust, 1733

" Full Organ, Old Style: Gedackt 16 ft., Prinzipal 8 ft., Oktav 4ft. Mixtur 6-10 ranks – without Sesquialtera or Rauschpfeife."

(A Quartane of two ranks: $2\frac{2}{3}$ ft. and 2 ft., giving a 'rustling' sound).

" Full Organ, New Style: Prinzipal, Oktaves, Quints, Tierces – can be made sharper ' with Tertian, Sesquialtera, Mixtures, Scharf, Zimbel and 16 ft. Quintaton or Gedackt or Rohrflöte.' Another tone-colour: Quintaton 16 ft. with Glöckleinton 2 ft."
J. Adlung: Musica Mechanica Organoedi and Anleitung zur Mus. Gelahrheit, 1768.

Although, unhappily, Silbermann abandoned the proper placement of and even the use of the Rückpositiv, he separated the tone-qualities of the manuals of his organs in the following terms, which hardly need translating:

1. Hauptwerk von grossen und gravitatischen Mensuren.
2. Oberwerk von scharfen und penetraten Mensuren.
3. Brustwerk von delikaten und lieblichen Mensuren.
4. Pedal von starken (strong) und durchdringenden (penetrating) Mensuren.

At Grosshartmannsdorf, where he built an organ in 1741, he left a notebook for the organist, in which he gave an account of suitable stop combinations. This is interesting, not because it necessarily throws any light on Bach's methods of registration, but because it gives *mélanges* of stops which pleased Silbermann who had impeccable taste where organ-tone was concerned.

The stops of this two-manual organ were *Hauptwerk* 1. Principal 8 ft.; 2. Quintaden 8 ft.; 3. Cornet 3 ranks; 4. Quinta 3 ft.; 5. Mixtur 4 ranks; 6. Octave 8 ft.; 7. Rohrflöte 8 ft.; 8. Spitzflöte 4 ft.; 9. Octava 2 ft. *Oberwerk.* 10. Gedackt 8 ft.; 11. Rohrflöte 4 ft.; 12. Nasat 3 ft.; 13 Octave 2 ft.; 14. Gemshorn 2 ft.; 15. Quinta 1⅓ ft.; 16. Cymbel 2 ranks; 17. Tertia 1⅗ ft.; 18. Sifflöte 1 ft.

Pedal. 19. Subbass 16 ft.; 20. Posaunenbass; 21. Octavbass 8 ft.; Bassventil; Tremulant.

" Pure " full organ.   1, 6, 7, 4, 9, 5, 10, 11, 13, 15, 18, 16, 19, 20, 21.
Flute combination: 7, 8, 10, 11.
" Sharp " flute combination: 10, 11, 18.
Soft flute combination: 2.8; 7.8; 1, 8, 10, 11, 14.
Cornet combination: 1, 7, 6, 3; 10, 11, 14 as accompaniment.
A softer cornet effect in the Oberwerk: 10, 12, 17 as a solo.
A nazard combination: 10, 11, 12 as a solo; 7, 8 as accompaniment.
A tertian combination: 10, 11, 12, 13, 17 as a solo melody.
Stahlspiel (a " steely " bell-tone): 10, 12, 15, 17 as a solo; 7, 8 as accompaniment.

STOPS IN BACH'S ORGANS

Barem (Old German: Bar—a song)

A flue stop with covered pipes, usually of 16 ft. or 8 ft. pitch. It had a pure, singing tone and was almost identical with the Stillgedeckt.

Bärpfeife (German: Bear-pipe)

An old regal stop with a gruff sound. Stops of the seventeenth-century and after with this name were sometimes flue stops of a flute character. It is possible that the etymology of the word was then to be found in that of Barem above.[1]

Bauernflöte (German: Peasant-flute)

A closed stop of small scale, found in German organs in 8 ft., 4 ft., 2 ft. and 1 ft. pitches. An 8 ft. example is found in the positiv division of the organ in the Jakobikirche, Hamburg.

Blockflöte (Plockflöte) (German: Recorder)

A metal flue stop of large scale, usually of 4 ft. pitch. Sometimes it has been found in 16 ft., 8 ft. and 2 ft. pitches also. The pipes may be open or stopped, cylindrical or conical in form. The stop was popular in Father Smith's English organs at the time of the birth of Bach.

Bombarde (French)

A reed stop, usually of 16 ft. pitch, and penetrating in tone. The power of the stop in the time of Bach was much less than might be expected from its name.

Bordun (German: Bourdon)

A closed manual stop usually of metal, of large scale and with a clear, flute-like tone. It had little relationship to the wooden pedal stops so popular in the twentieth-century.

Chalumeau (French) *Schalmei* (German)

A soft-toned reed stop intended to imitate the old instrument called the schawm or schalmei, a precursor of the clarinet. It is found in 16 ft., 8 ft. and 4 ft. pitches. The stop was of great utility both on manual and pedal. It would blend with a flue chorus and had interesting solo possibilities both alone and in combination with other stops.

Ciflet. See Sifflöte.

Cilinderquinte

A quint (2⅔′) stop with small-scaled cylindrical tubes.

Cimbel. See Cymbel.

---

[1] The Dutch baarpijp is a flue stop of conical construction.

Coppel (Koppel) (Copula) 1

A mechanical device for connecting one manual with another, or a manual with the pedals.

Coppel (Koppel) 2

A neutral-toned flue stop of 8 ft. pitch, which was used as a fundamental tone for joining other tones together, or for erecting " tonal pyramids " by the addition of ranks of mutation harmonics. The pipes were usually of spindle shape, with inverted cones at the top.

Cornet

A stop composed of wide-scale pipes with individual dull-tone; the separate ranks being 8 ft., 4 ft., 2⅔ ft., 2 ft., and 1⅗ ft. The synthesised tone is not unlike that of a reed. Normally, there were no breaks in the ranks, but sometimes the bass of the stop was made of fewer ranks. The baroque cornets were made of a heavily-leaded metal to secure a dull flute-like tone in each rank. Cornet stops of quiet intonation were made for the positiv sections of the instruments, in addition to the loud cornets of the Hauptwerk.

Cornettin. Cornet bass (Corneto)

A reed of 4 ft. or 2 ft., usually found on the pedal organ (as at Arnstadt) and useful in pedal solos, as well as for giving brightness to the pedal tone. The pipes were of small scale with broad, thin tongues, and of inverted conical shape.

Cremona

A corruption of Krummhorn. It has no relation to the Cremona Violin.

Cymbel, Zymbel (German)

A high-pitched mixture usually breaking at every octave. The ranks should be alternatively octave- and fifth-sounding.

Cymbelstern (German: Cymbel-star)

One or more large wooden and gilded " stars " in a prominent part of the organ case. When the stop was drawn a wind motor caused the star to turn and small bells or " jingles " at the points were sounded one after another. The bells gave the tonic and dominant; tonic, mediant, dominant, tonic; or the notes of the scale.

Diapason (Greek—from the first to the last note)

A moderate-scaled open metal stop of 8 ft. pitch. Not often found in German organs.

Dulzian. (German: *Dulcian*)

A reed stop of 8 ft. or 16 ft. tone found on both manuals and pedals, of tone not unlike that of the bassoon, but sweeter and broader in tone. Occasionally flue-pipes were used, of cylindrical or outward-tapering pattern.

Fagotto (Italian)

A *mf* reed stop of bassoon tone. The tubes are slender and conical in form. The stop is useful on both manuals and pedals and is found in 16 ft., and less often 8 ft., pitch.

Feldpfeife (German: Military Flute)

An open flue stop of penetrating flute tone. The pipes have high mouths. The pitch is 4 ft., 2 ft. or 1 ft. The stop has never been a favourite, as the tone is intense and assertive.

Flachflöte (German: " Flat " Flute)

Originally the pipes were of wood and were flat in form with the mouth on a wide side. At the time of Bach, the stop was usually made of metal pipes of gemshorn character or of spindle shape. The pitch of the stop was usually 4 ft., and it had a distinctive flute character in addition to good blending properties.

Flageolet

An open metal stop of 2 ft. or 1 ft. pitch with clear and penetrating tone. The word *l'arigot* is derived from flageolet, but then it is a nineteenth, 1⅓ ft. (The flageolet in the organ at St. Bavon's Church, Haarlem, is of 1⅓ ft. pitch).

Fugara (Bohemian=German: Hirtenflöte; a shepherd's pipe of reedy intonation)

This flue stop is of wood or metal, and is in 8 ft. or 4 ft. pitch. Its tone is usually a combination of string and horn, but sometimes it has just a cutting gamba-tone.

Gedackt (Gedeckt, Gedacht) (German)

A stopped flue pipe of wood or metal. (In North German organs it was usually of metal). It corresponds to the old English stopped diapason, but it is usually of smaller scale and the odd harmonics are more noticeable in its voice.

Gedackte italienische Quinte (German)

A fifth sounding rank of stopped pipes. At the time of Bach the " Italian " stops were of wide scale and blended very well with other such stops. (The sixteenth- and early seventeenth-century Italian stops were probably of small scale).

Gemshorn (literally goat or chamois horn)

A metal open stop, tapering though not so acutely as the Spitzflöte, in 4 ft., 2 ft. (and more rarely 8 ft.) pitches.

Glockenspiel (German: bell music)

Originally a short compass set of tuned dish-shaped bells, spiral rods, bars or tubes of bell-metal sounded by hammers. The stop was sometimes made by Arp Schnitger. It was used at Christmas, New Year and Easter festivals. The pitch of the bells was usually 4 ft.

Grob (Gros, Grosse), e.g. Grobgedackt

A large-scaled covered flue-stop.

Grosse-Hall Quinta

A large-scale and powerful Quinta of 5⅓ ft. pitch.

Helle-Cymbel (German: Helle=Bright)

A very bright-toned cymbel mixture, usually breaking at every octave.

Hohlflöte (German: hohl=hollow)

A hollow-toned flute properly made with open wooden pipes. Examples with wide-scaled stopped metal pipes are known.

Klein (German: small)

A prefix indicating that the stop is of 4 ft. pitch or that the scale of the pipes is small.

Kornett. See Cornet.

Krummhorn, Krumbhorn (German: crooked or bent horn) (French: Cromorne)

A reed stop of 8 ft. or 4 ft. pitch of soft tone. The tubes are cylindrical and the tone is not unlike that of the clarinet. The old orchestral krummhorn was bent, at its lower end, in the form of a half circle, and had six finger holes.

Largo (Larigot) (French: L'arigot=a flageolet)

An important mutation stop of soft tone and 1⅓ ft. pitch. It is useful in blending with other stops to give quiet, piquant tones.

Lieblich gedackt (German: lovely, covered)

An 8 ft. wood or metal flue stop with stopped-pipes and of beautiful quality. Its scale is usually somewhat smaller than that of the gedackt.

Mixtur (Mixture)

Originally the high-pitched ranks of octave and fifth-sounding pipes which remained when the pipe-ranks of graver pitch had been given individual control by the use of the slider chest. The true organ mixtur contains only octave and fifth sounding ranks. As it is not desirable, even though it were possible, to carry very acute ranks throughout the scale, breaks in the composition of the mixture ranks occur several times in the course of the compass of the keyboard.

Mixtures not only give brilliance to the smaller scaled flue work, but because of their breaks they give depth to the treble of the compass, clarity in the middle, and definition and brilliance in the bass. They also bind the flue work with the reed tones. Mixtures are an essential part of the tonal equipment of even small organs of not more than a dozen registers. In the seventeenth and eighteenth centuries, mixtures were found on each of the manuals and on the pedals. When organs were tuned to equal temperament, the numerous slight dissonances between the true intervals of the mixture ranks and the tempered intervals of the fundamental tones of the scale gave the organ tone its unique scintillation. (This was, of course, no new sound as slight departures from consonance would have produced the same effect before this time).

Analyses of some Mixture Stops (given in pitches)

4-6 rank Hauptwerk Mixture (Arp Schnitger)

C	$1'$	$\frac{2}{3}'$	$\frac{1}{2}'$	$\frac{1}{3}'$		
c	$1\frac{1}{3}'$	$1'$	$1\frac{1}{3}'$	$\frac{1}{2}'$		
c^1	$2'$	$1\frac{1}{3}'$	$1'$	$\frac{2}{3}'$		
c^2	$2'$	$1\frac{1}{3}'$	$1'$	$\frac{2}{3}'$	$\frac{2}{3}'$	
c^3	$4'$	$2\frac{2}{3}'$	$2'$	$2'$	$1\frac{1}{3}'$	$1\frac{1}{3}'$

5 rank Hauptwerk Mixture (G. Silbermann)

C	$2'$	$1\frac{1}{3}'$	$1'$	$\frac{2}{3}'$	$\frac{1}{2}'$
c	$2\frac{2}{3}'$	$2'$	$1\frac{1}{3}'$	$1'$	$\frac{2}{3}'$
c^1	$4'$	$2\frac{2}{3}'$	$2'$	$1\frac{1}{3}'$	$1'$
c^2	$8'$	$4'$	$2\frac{2}{3}'$	$2'$	$1\frac{1}{3}'$
c^3	$8'$	$8'$	$4'$	$2\frac{2}{3}'$	$2'$

Mutation (Latin: change)

A stop which changes the note, i.e. not a unison or suboctave or octave-sounding stop. Thus a 2 ft. stop is not strictly a mutation; but a nazard $2\frac{2}{3}$ ft. which sounds a *g* when a *c* is played, or a tierce which sounds an *e* when *c* is played is a mutation. The word is now used loosely for all separate ranks above 4 ft. pitch which can be combined together to make " tonal pyramids."

Nachthorn (German) (French: Cor de Nuit) (Night horn)

A large-scaled but fairly quiet, closed metal flue-stop, with a slightly horn tone. The tone is an interesting combination of " stopped flute " and " soft French horn."

Nassat. Nasat (German) (French: nasard, nazard) $2\frac{2}{3}$ ft.

An important mutation stop of flute tone giving the twelfth above the note played. It is most useful in combination and gives a piquant flavour to other tones of graver pitch.

Octav (Oktave)

The correct name for the octave to any principal rank, whatever the pitch, i.e. the octave to a 4 ft. Principal would be a 2 ft. rank, etc.

Pauke

A drum—usually a kettle drum. (Sometimes it was played with mechanical action by an " angel " in the casework).

Praestant (Latin: Prae-stans—standing before, or in front)

An open metal (octav) stop which, strictly speaking, stood in the front, i.e. in the case, with the organ Principal (prinzipal).

Prinzipal or *Principal*

An open metal stop, which denoted the pitch of the division of the organ of which it was the " unison " representative of the open-flue " male-chorus." Thus the principal would be found in 32 ft., 16 ft. (pedal, hauptwerk), 8 ft. (hauptwerk, positiv), 4 ft. (positiv, brustwerk, oberwerk) pitches. It was not so loud, but brighter and usually harder in quality than an English great-organ open diapason.

Some Scales (*Pipe Diameters of Principals in inches*)

	C	c	c¹	c²	c³
Schnitger					
(Hauptwerk 8 ft.)	5.8	3.65	1.95	1.12	0.75
(Hauptwerk 4 ft.)	2.95	1.75	1.00	.62	0.37
Silbermann					
(Hauptwerk 8 ft.)	6.40	3.45	1.90	1.10	0.64
(Hauptwerk 4 ft.)	3.45	1.90	1.10	0.64	0.40
Diapason (*English* 19th *c.*)					
Medium Scale	5.56	3.30	1.96	1.16	0.69
Large Scale	6.60	3.93	2.33	1.39	0.82

Posaune (German)

A reed stop, usually of 16 ft. pitch on the pedals and 8 ft. pitch on the manuals. The posaune is intended to copy the tone of the trombone as far as possible. In the seventeenth- and eighteenth-century organs the lower wind pressure did not permit the loudness which is a feature of the modern stop of that name. The old posaune was, nevertheless, usually the loudest stop on the instrument; its tone may be described as " thin trumpet". Such stops as made by Silbermann had more body and depth of tone than had the North German examples.

Querflöte (German) (Traverse- or cross-flute)

A small-scaled flute intended to imitate the tone of the orchestral flute. The pipes are made of wood or metal, but oak or peartree-wood pipes of small scale gave good results.

Quinta decima (Latin) (A fifteenth)

A 2 ft. stop, usually of quiet flute or " principal " tone.

Quintadena

The pipes are of closed metal, and the twelfth is very prominent in the tone. The stop is of considerable antiquity, and was known at the end of the fifteenth century. It is usually found in 8 ft. and 4 ft. pitches.

Quintaten (Latin: Quintam tenentes—holding the fifth)

This stop is not fundamentally different from that above. (The Latin name is now of more common usage than the German above). The pitches are usually 16 ft., 8 ft. and 4 ft.

Ranket (Racket, Rankett)

An old regal stop in which the reeds were qualified by short resonators. The tone which is not unlike that of a coarse harmonium reed was supposed to imitate the tone of the sixteenth-century wind instrument, the ranket. Very occasionally flue-pipes were used.

Rauschpfeife (Rauschflöte) (German—rustling pipe or flute)

A compound stop with open metal flute ranks of 2 ft. and 1⅓ ft. pitch respectively.

Rauschquint (German: rustling quint)

A two-rank open metal compound stop with pitches of 2⅔ ft. and 2 ft. respectively. The interval between the ranks was a fourth, and the stop has been called Quarta or recently Quartane. It is a pleasant, quiet mixture which imparts a gentle rustling to the flue tone as distinct from the reediness of the sesquialtera.

Regal (Latin: regulo—to regulate or give the notes for the singing (?))

An old reed stop. Small resonators of divers shapes were fitted to qualify the tones of the vibrating tongues. Regals were sometimes named after the shapes of these resonators thus: apfel-, knop- (kop), trichter-regals (apple, knob or head, funnel regals respectively), or according to their tones: singend-, harfen-, geigen-, gedampft-regals (singing-, harp-, violin-, subdued-regals respectively). The regal was also the earliest (fifteenth-century) portable reed organ or reed portative. The flue-pipe portatives came at an earlier date.

The regals, if in tune, gave a pleasant body and colour to combinations of flue tones. They were often used alone for accompanying the voice.

Rohrflöte (German: flute with tubes)

A wide-scaled metal stop in which each pipe is covered by canisters, to a hole in the top of which is soldered a length of open metal tube. Although various makeshift devices, such as perforated wooden stoppers instead of the tubes, have been used, the interesting, slightly piquant flute-tone can only be obtained by the original construction. The tone is at once definite, clear and singing, and the upper partials generated in the tube give it great individuality. It is commonly an 8 ft. stop.

Salicional (Latin: Salix—a willow)

A very narrow-scaled open metal 8 ft. flue stop with a soft, refined tone which has a slight stringiness or reediness in its voice.

Schalmei, Schallmey (German)

See Chalumeau.

Scharf

A sharp mixture of brilliant tone. It often contained a high-pitched 3rd-sounding-rank, which helped to give it a penetrating quality. A four rank stop might start with 15th, 17th, 19th and 22nd.

Schweizer Flöte (German: Swiss flute)

An open metal stop of 8 ft., 4 ft., 2 ft. or even 1 ft. pitch; a hybrid between string and flute.

Sedecima (Latin abbreviation)

A seventeenth or tierce 1⅗ ft. pitch.

Sertin (Serpent?)

A reed stop of 8 ft. or 16 ft. pitch intended to imitate the old orchestral instrument which had a tone between those of the bassoon and the trumpet, and was made with a curious " wriggling " shape. It was part of the cornett family, in which the cornett or zink was the alto or tenor, the serpent the bass, and the cornettino (corneto) the soprano instrument. It is possible that the name is a corruption of Sourdine – a soft reed.

Sesquialtera (Sexquialtera)

A compound stop of two ranks; the twelfth 2⅔ ft. and the tierce 1⅗ ft., giving the interval of a sixth. Sometimes other ranks were added. The sesquialtera, which is *not* a part of the " male " principal choruses, gives a reedy quality rather than to brilliance to other flue tones. A " cornet " can be made by adding further large-scale ranks of harmonics to the sesquialtera. The stop was originally so-called because its two ranks suggested the " one to one and a half " or 2 : 3 ratio.

Sifflöte, Sifflet (German: whistle-flute)

A small open-metal flute stop of medium scale and of 2 ft. or even 1 ft. pitch.

Sperrventil (German: literally, a wind block)

A valve for shutting off the wind from a particular wind-chest.

Spielpfeiffe

Literally, a musical pipe, but probably the word is a corruption of spillpfeiffe (*q.v.*).

Spillflöte, spillpfeiffe (German: Spindel flöte=spindle flute)

An 8 ft., 4 ft. or 2 ft. stop with spindle-shaped metal flue pipes, i.e. a conical foot with a cylindrical body surmounted by an inverted cone. It has a distinctive and beautiful tone with characteristic harmonics. It is sometimes made nowadays, particularly in America. Often it has a tone like that of the schwiegel.

Spitzflöte (German: spire flute)

An open metal stop of 8 ft., 4 ft. or 2 ft. pitch with a tapering pipe not unlike that of the gemshorn but with a taper of ratio lower end to top diameters of 3 : 1. The tone is bright and clear, but a trace of the seventeenth in its voice gives it a slightly incisive quality of tone. It is a most useful stop when used separately or in combination.

Stillgedeckt (Still-gedackt) (German: literally, a quiet-toned, covered stop)

A soft lieblich gedackt, usually of wood, and of 8 ft. or 4 ft. pitch.

Tertia

A name sometimes given to a tierce or terz (*q.v.*), or a corruption of tertian or terzian (*q.v.*).

Tertian, terzian

A two rank compound stop of open metal pipes of medium scale which stand at the interval of a minor third apart, and so give the stop its name. It may be regarded as an inversion of the sesquialtera. When the stop belongs to the 8 ft. harmonic series it is composed of ranks of $1\frac{3}{5}$ ft. and $1\frac{1}{3}$ ft. pitch. The stop gives breadth and a slight reediness, rather than brilliance, to other flue combinations. It also has interesting solo possibilities whether used alone or in combination with other stops.

Terz, tierce, tritonus

An important mutation stop of $1\frac{3}{5}$ ft. pitch, when it is part of the 8 ft. harmonic series; or of $3\frac{1}{5}$ ft. when it is part of the 16 ft. series. It is a moderate-scale metal stop often of gemshorn tone. It imparts a pleasant reediness to other flue tones, and is a useful constituent of synthetic solo reed tones.

Traversa

A traverse-flute.

Tremulant

A mechanical device for imparting a wave to the organ tone by interfering with the wind supply in a cyclic manner. In old organs there were two types of tremulant; those which imparted a gentle wave or hovering to the tone: hence the German name Schwebung for this device. The other tremulant was more violent in its effects and as it depended for its action on " lost-wind " the tone was practically shut off during each cycle. In the time of Bach, adjustable tremulants and those which gave compound beats, e.g. in triple time, were known. The tremulant is of considerable antiquity, and was highly esteemed in the sixteenth and seventeenth centuries.

Trichter Regal

A regal (reed) stop with short funnel-shaped resonators.

Trommel

Drum with mechanical action. (Not to be confused with trommet).

Trommet, Trompete, Tromete, etc. (German: a trumpet)

A reed stop with long conical resonators, giving a *mf* or *f* tone rich in harmonics. The trumpet stops formed the reed culmination of the " male " or small-scaled chorus. The pitch was 8 ft. or 16 ft. The seventeenth- and eighteenth-century trumpets were of modest power when compared with modern examples.

Untersatz (German: sitting under, foundation)

A pedal stop of 32 ft. pitch and usually made of stopped wooden pipes, placed on a separate chest on or near the floor (hence the name). The stop would now be called sub-bourdon.

Ventile (*Ventil*)

See Sperrventil.

Vigesima Nona (Latin derivation)

A nineteenth or larigot 1⅓ ft., but sometimes given as 1½ ft. in pitch.

Viol di (*da*) *Gamba* (Italian)

A broad-toned string stop supposed to be imitative of the old viol, which was held between the legs. At the time of Bach it was often of slow speech and needed the help of another flue-stop, such as a coppel, to secure prompt attack. It was used by E. Compenius as early as 1610.

Vogelgesang (German: bird-song)

One or more open metal pipes of small scale were bent round so that the open ends could be immersed below the surface of water in a pot. It was necessary to keep the pot filled with water in order to maintain the bird " in song".

Violon (Violone)

An open flue-stop usually of 16 ft. pitch and of fairly small or moderate scale, of wood or metal. When properly made, the stop has a firm, definite tonality, which endeavours to imitate that of the double-bass.

Vox Humana

A member of the " schnarrwerk " or regal class. Usually short cylindrical resonators qualify the tones of free or beating reeds. At the time of Bach (and before this) various shapes of resonator tube were used to imitate various vowel sounds. The Vox Humana is a useful timbre-creator.

Waldflöte (German: Forest Flute)

An open-flute, of large scale wood or metal types, and found in 8 ft., 4 ft., and more rarely 2 ft. and 1 ft., pitches. In later years it became a favourite stop in 4 ft. pitch of English organ builders.

Waldhorn (German: forest or hunting horn)

A reed stop of 8 ft. and 4 ft. (and more recently of 16 ft.) pitch of fairly smooth tone. Many of the older specimens had a tonal quality resembling that of a clarinet.

References

C. Mahrenholz: *Die Orgelregister: ihre Geschichte und ihr Bau* (Kassel, 1930).
W. L. Sumner: *The Organ: its Evolution, Principles of Construction and Use* (London, 1952).

THE COMPASSES OF BACH'S ORGANS

The following table gives the manual and pedal compasses of the chief organs which were played by Bach. No doubt he was limited by the resources of particular organs when he played his own compositions on them. There is textual evidence that he could not always carry out his intentions in some of his larger organ works because of the limitations of the compass.

In an important article Emery points out the difficulties of using the compasses of Bach's organ for fixing the dates of his works without other evidence.[1] The textual history of many works cannot be established with the necessary precision; and transposed copies were sometimes found.

	Number of Stops	Manual	Pedal	Keyboard Compass	
				Manual	Pedal
1. Arnstadt, Bonifaciuskirche	23	2	1	C, D, E–d³	C, D, E–d¹
2. Mühlhausen, St. Blasiuskirche (after rebuild)	37	3	1	C, D–d³	C, D–d¹
3. Weimar, Schlosskirche (a) Compenius-Organ	21	2	1	C, D, D♯, E, F, –c³	C, D, D♯, E, F–e¹ (without d♯¹)
(b) Rebuilt Organ	24	2	1	C–c³	C–d¹
4. Weissenfels, Augustusburg	30	2	1	C, D–c³	C, D–f¹
5. Köthen, Agnuskirche	28	2	1	C, D–d³ (e³, f³)	C, D–d¹, e¹, f¹
6. Köthen, Schlosskapelle	13	2	1	C–e³	C–e¹
7. Hamburg, Katharinenkirche	58	4	1	C, D, E, F, G, A–c³	C, D, E, F, F♯, G, A–d¹
8. Leipzig Organs: Thomaskirche Nikolaikirche Paulinerkirche	35 36 53	3 3 3	1 1 1	C, D–c³	C, D–d¹

after Werner David

[1] W. Emery: " The Compass of Bach's organs as evidence of the date of his works."—*The Organ*, xxxii, No. 126, 1952.

PART TWO

BACH'S ORGAN WORKS
WITH THE BWV NUMBERING

BIBLIOGRAPHY

INDEX — Page 65

BACH'S ORGAN WORKS
WITH THE BWV NUMBERING

A Concordance showing the relation of the Numbers of the Peters Urtext Edition in 9 volumes to the Schmieder BWV Numbers.

" a," " b " and " c " refer to the three different editions of Volume IX. In " a " and " b " the Chorale Preludes were numbered as a set, 9 and 12 respectively, and the individual Chorale Preludes had subsidiary Numbers as shown. In " c " each Chorale Prelude is numbered individually. The page references in Volume IX have been omitted to save complication.

Edition " a " is the first of Volume IX, by Ferdinand A. Roitzsch of 1881.

Edition " b " is the revision of the former by Max Seiffert of 1904.

Edition " c " is the (current) edition by Hermann Keller.

I. THE FREE ORGAN WORKS
compiled by F. F. Clough and G. J. Cuming

The durations given are part of "A list of Durations and Associated Data of Bach's Works," by J. H. Davies, Music Librarian, B.B.C., contained in Hinrichsen's Seventh Music Book (now out of print). The blank spaces may be used to fill in the missing durations.

" d " indicates works called by Schmieder " Prelude and Fugue".

" e " indicates listing by Schmieder among the works for Clavier.

" f " indicates that the work referred to is included in " Bach's Art of Part-Playing," by Stainton de B. Taylor (P.E. No. 350k), containing also other Trios.

Title	Peters Edition Volume	Number	BWV	Duration
ALLABREVE, D major	VIII	6	589	
ARIA, F major	IX	8(a); 11(b); 5(c): 5(f)	587	
(Transcription of Couperin: Courante II, from *La Françoise*)				
CANZONA, D minor	IV	10	588	
CONCERTOS				
1. G major, after Johann Ernst v. Sachsen-Weimar	VIII	1	592	
2. A minor, after Vivaldi Op. 3 No. 8	VIII	2	593	10'30"
3. C major, after Vivaldi Op. 7 No. 11, D major	VIII	3	594	

Title	Peters Edition		BWV	Duration
	Volume	Number		
4. C major, after Johann Ernst v. Sachsen-Weimar	VIII	4	595	
5. D minor, after Vivaldi Op. 3 No. 11	Separately (P.E. 3002)		596	
6. E flat major (Vivaldi, previously attributed to W. F. Bach) ..	IX	7 (b only)	597	
DUETTOS [740] (P.E. 4465) ..			802-5(e)	9'
FANTASIAS				
C major (Andreas Bach Book) ..	VIII	9	570	
C major (unfinished)	[Clavierbüchlein]		573	
C minor (unfinished fugue?) ..	IV	12	562	4'30"
G major, 5th Concerto (doubtful)	IX	6(a,b); 4(c)	571	
G major (3 movements)	IV	11	572	7'30"
B minor, *Con imitazione* ..	XIII (Clavier) 7 / IX (Organ) 1 (c only)		563	
FANTASIAS AND FUGUES				
C minor, *Great*	III	6	537 (d)	9'
C minor (unfinished fugue?) ..	IV	12	562	
G minor, *Great*	II	4	542 (d)	9'
A minor	IX	1(a,b); 6(c)	561	
FUGUES (see also Fantasias & Fugues, Preludes & Fugues, and Toccatas & Fugues)				
C major, *Hexachord*	VIII	10	946(e)	
C major (doubtful)	[BG XXXVIII Anh. 2(i)] Anh. 90			
C minor, *Legrenzi or Double Fugue*	IV	6	574	
C minor (attrib. C. P. E. Bach) ..	IV	9	575	
D major (doubtful)	IX	5(a,b only)	580	
D minor, *Giant*	VII	60	680	
E minor, *Wedge* or *Scissors*, or *Great*	II	9	548	
G major, ...	IX	2(a,b); 7(c)	576	
G major, *à la Gigue*	IX	4(a,b); 2(c)	577	3'30"
G minor, *Little* or *Folk Song* ..	IV	7	578	3'30"
G minor (from Cantata 131) ..	VIII	12	131a	
B minor, on a theme of Corelli Op. 3 No. 4	IV	8	579	5'30"
G major	[Steingräber 2173]		581	
KLEINES HARMONISCHES LABYRINTH, C major (attrib. Heinichen)	IX	3(a,b): 9(c)	591	
ORGELBÜCHLEIN (Little Organ Book), see section B			599-644	
PASSACAGLIA AND FUGUE, C minor	I	7	582	12'
PASTORALE, F major (4 mvts.) ..	I	8	590	
PEDAL-EXERCITIUM, G minor	IX	11 (c only)	598	
PRELUDES				
C major (doubtful)	VIII	8	567	
C major (manuals only)	VIII	7	943 (e)	
G major	VIII	11	568	
A minor	IV	13	569	

Title	Peters Edition Volume	Number	BWV	Dura-tion
PRELUDES AND FUGUES				
8 Short Preludes and Fugues ..	VIII	5	553-560	
C major, *Trumpet*	IV	1	531	5′30″
C major, *Weimar*	II	1	545	
(an earlier form of the Prelude)			545a)	
C major, *Leipzig*	II	7	547	8′
C minor, *Arnstadt*	IV	5	549	5′
C minor	II	6	546	
C minor, *Great*	III	6	537	9′
D major	IV	3	532	10′
(an earlier form of the Fugue)			532a)	
D minor, Fugue from Violin Solo Sonata 1 (*Fiddle*)	III	4	539	
E flat major, *St. Anne*, or *Trinity*	III	1	552	13′
E minor, *Short, Cathedral* or *Nightwatchman* ..	III	10	533	4′30″
E minor, *Wedge* or *Scissors* ..	II	9	548	15′
F minor	II	5	534	9′
G major	IV	2	550	8′
G major, *Great*	II	2	541	6′30″
G minor	III	5	535	
A major	II	3	536	6′
A minor	III	9	551	
A minor, *Great*	II	8	543	9′
B minor, *Great* or *The Sands of Time*	II	10	544	10′30″
SONATAS ("Trio Sonatas")			525-530	
1. E flat major	I	1	525	12′
2. C minor	I	2	526	10′
3. D minor	I	3	527	12′
4. E minor	I	4	528	11′30″
5. C major	I	5	529	14′
6. G major	I	6	530	11′
TOCCATAS AND FUGUES				
C major (or E major)	III	7	566	
C major (Toccata, with a long Pedal Cadenza, Adagio and Fugue)	III	8	564	15′
D minor	IV	4	565	9′
D minor, *Dorian*	III	3	538 (d)	9′
E major: see above.				
F major (*Colossal* or *Tremendous*)	III	2	540 (d)	13′
TRIOS (See also under Aria and Sonatas above)				
C minor (doubtful—? Krebs) ..	IX	7(a); 9(b); 10(c); 3(f)	585	
D minor	IV	14; 4(f)	583	
G major (from Gamba Sonata No. 1)	IX	8(b); 3(c); 2(f)	1027a	
G major (really by Telemann) ..	IX	10(b); 8(c); 1(f)	586	
G minor	[Bach Jahrbuch, 1909]		584	

II. WORKS, BASED ON CHORALES
with Title translations revised by Gordon Phillips

Bach constructed 143 authentic Organ movements on 77 melodies from the Lutheran liturgy: 46 in *Orgelbuechlein*, 17 in Part III of *Clavieruebung*, 18 in *The Eighteen Chorales*, 6 in the *Schuebler Chorales*, 4 in Variations and Partitas, 52 in miscellaneous and ungrouped Preludes.

In the light of modern scholarship and ideas, many of the English Titles of Bach's Organ Works based on Chorales seem to be due for revision. Some of the English names which have long been used are quite acceptable; others are free translations, misleading in some cases when compared with the original text.

For example, the well-known Chorale Prelude " Jesu meine Freude," often receives the English title " Jesu Priceless Treasure," whereas the meaning of the original German is " Jesu, my Joy," or again " Schmücke dich, o liebe Seele " is translated " Deck thyself, my soul, with gladness," although the true meaning of the words is "Adorn thyself, beloved soul."

These English title revisions have been made with the object of providing not only an accurate version, but one which is also fitting to the sense and dignity of the German titles, and metrically pleasing to the ear.

GERMAN		ENGLISH	VOL.	NUMBER	PAGE	BWV
Ach bleib' bei uns, Herr Jesu Christ	(Sch 5)	O stay with us, Lord Jesus Christ	VI	2	4	649
Ach Gott und Herr (also attributed to Walther)		O God and Lord	VI	1	3	693
idem		idem	IX	9-i (a only)		692
idem		idem	IX	9-ii (a) 12-i (b) 12 (c)		714
Ach Gott vom Him- mel sieh darein		O Lord, from Heaven	IX	9-vi (a) 12-vii (b) 13 (c)		741
Ach Herr, mich armen Sünder		O Lord, poor Sinner that I am	IX	12-xiv (b)		742
Ach was ist doch unser Leben		Alas, what is this Life of ours?	IX	12-xv (b)		743
Ach was soll ich Sünder machen (Partita)			IX	26 (c)		770
Ach wie nichtig, ach wie flüchtig	(OB 45)	O how empty, O how fleeting	V	1	2	644
Alle Menschen müs- sen sterben	(OB 44)	All Men are mortal	V	2	2	643
Allein Gott in der Höh' sei Ehr'	(CU 7)	All Glory be to God on high	VI	5	10	675
*idem	(CU 8)	idem	VI	6	12	676
idem (Fughetta)	(CU 9)	idem	VI	10	29	677
idem	(E 12)	idem	VI	9	26	662
*idem	(E 13)	idem	VI	8	22	663
*idem (Trio)	(E 14)	idem	VI	7	17	664
idem (Bicinium)		idem	VI	3	6	711
idem		idem	VI	4	8	717
idem (Fuga)		idem	VI	11	30	716
idem		idem	IX	14 (c)		715

†D

German	English	Vol.	Number	Page	BWV
*An Wasserflüssen Babylon (E 3)	By the Waters of Babylon	VI	12b	34	653
idem	idem	VI	12a	32	653b
Auf meinen lieben Gott	To my beloved God	IX	{ 9iii (a), 12ii (b), 15 (c) }		744
Aus der Tiefe rufe ich	Out of the Depths I cry (De Profundis)	IX	{ 9x (a), 12xi (b), 16 (c) }		745
Aus tiefer Noth schrei' ich zu dir (CU 18)	In deepest need I cry to Thee	VI	13	36	686
idem (CU 19)	idem	VI	14	38	687
Christ, der du bist der helle Tag (Partita)	Christ, Thou art the bright Day	V-2	1	60	766
Christ ist erstanden (OB 29)	Christ is risen	V	4	4	627
Christ lag in Todesbanden (OB 27)	Christ lay in the Bonds of Death	V	5	7	625
idem	idem	VI	15	40	718
*idem (Fantasie)	idem	VI	16	43	695
idem (actually by Pachelbel)	idem	IX	9xi (a)		Anh. 171
Christ unser Herr zum Jordan kam (CU 16)	Christ our Lord to Jordan came	VI	17	46	684
idem (CU 17)	idem	VI	18	49	685
Christe, aller Welt Trost (CU 2)	Christ, Consolation of the World	VII	39b	20	670
idem (CU 5)	idem	VII	40b	27	673
Christe, du Lamm Gottes (OB 21)	Christ, Thou Lamb of God	V	3	3	619
Christum, wir sollen loben schon (OB 13)	To Christ we now give praise	V	6	8	611
Christum wir sollen loben schon or Was fürcht'st du (Fughetta)	To Christ we now give praise or Why dreadest thou	V	7	9	696
*Christus, der uns selig macht (OB 22)	Christ, who makes us blissful	V	8	10	620
idem	idem	IX	12xviii (b)		747
Da Jesus an dem Kreuze stund' (OB 23)	When Jesus hung upon the Cross	V	9	11	621
Das alte Jahr vergangen ist (OB 16)	The old Year now has passed away	V	10	12	614
Das Jesulein soll doch mein Trost	In Christ alone my Comfort is	IX	{ 9vii (a), 12viii (b), 17 (c) }		702
Der Tag, der ist so freudenreich (OB 7)	O Day, so rich in gladness	V	11	13	605
Dies sind die heil'gen zehn Gebot' (OB 36)	These are the ten Holy Commandments	V	12	14	635
idem (CU 10)	idem	VI	19	50	678
idem (Fughetta) (CU 11)	idem	VI	20	54	679
Durch Adams Fall ist ganz verderbt (OB 38)	Through Adam's Fall, Mankind is lost	V	13	15	637
idem (Fuga)	idem	VI	21	56	705
Ein' feste Burg ist unser Gott	A safe stronghold our God is still or A mighty Fortress is our God	VI	22	58	720
Erbarm' dich mein, o Herre Gott	Have mercy on me, Lord	—	—	—	—
Erschienen ist der herrliche Tag (OB 31)	The glorious Day has now appeared	V	15	17	629
Erstanden ist der heil'ge Christ (OB 30)	Arisen is the Holy Christ	V	14	16	628
Es ist das Heil uns 'kommen her (OB 39)	Salvation unto us has come	V	16	18	638

GERMAN	ENGLISH	VOL.	NUMBER	PAGE	BWV
Gelobet seist du, Jesu Christ (OB 6)	Praised be Thou, O Jesus Christ				
idem (Fughetta)	idem	V	17	19	604
idem	idem	V	18	20	697
idem	idem	V-Anh.	1	102	722
idem	idem	VI	23	61	723
*Gott der Vater, wohn' uns bei	God the Father, stay with us	VI	24	62	748
Gott, durch deine Güte or Gottes Sohn ist kommen (OB 2)	God by thy Goodness The Son of God is come	V	19	20	600
Gottes Sohn ist kommen (Fughetta)		V	20	22	703
idem	idem	VI	25	64	724
Helft mir Gottes Güte preisen (OB 15)	Help me to praise the Goodness of God	V	21	23	613
Herr Christ, der ein'ge Gottes Sohn or Herr Gott, nun sei gepreiset (OB 3)	Lord Christ, the only Son of God	V	22	24	601
idem (Fughetta)	idem	V	23	25	698
Herr Gott, dich loben wir	Lord God, we praise Thee	VI	26	65	725
Herr Gott, nun schleuss' den Himmel auf (OB 19)	Lord God, now open Heaven's Gate	V	24	26	617
Herr Gott, nun sei gepreiset (OB 3)	Now we praise God Almighty	V	22	24	601
Herr Jesu Christ, dich zu uns wend' (OB 34)	Lord Jesus Christ, turn Thou to us	V	25	28	632
idem	idem	V	26	28	709
*idem (E 5)	idem	VI	27	70	655
idem	idem	IX	18 (c)		726
Herzlich tut mich verlangen	I long with all my heart	V	27	30	727
Heut triumphieret Gottes Sohn (OB 32)	The Son of God prevails to-day	V	28	30	630
Hilf, Gott, dass mir's gelinge (OB 26)	God, help me to succeed	V	29	32	624
Ich hab' mein' Sach' Gott heimgestellt	I put my Case before the Lord	VI	28 (With Chorale)	74	707
Ich ruf' zu dir, Herr Jesu Christ (OB 40)	I call to Thee, Lord Jesus Christ	V	30	33	639
In dich hab' ich gehoffet, Herr (OB 41)	I have placed my Hope in Thee, O Lord	V	33	35	640
idem (Fughetta)	idem	VI	34	94	712
In dir ist Freude (OB 17)	In Thee is Joy	V	34	36	615
In dulci jubilo (OB 10)	Now sing, we, now rejoice	V	35	38	608
idem	idem	V-Anh.	2	103	729
idem	idem	IX	12xii (b) 19 (c)		751
Jesu, der du meine Seele hast ... herausgerissen	Jesu, Who hast saved my Soul	IX	12iii (b)		752
Jesu Leiden, Pein und Tod (by J. C. Vogler)	Jesu, suffering Pain and Death	IX	9-v (a)		Anh.57
Jesu, meine Freude (OB 12)	Jesu, my Joy	V	31	34	610
*idem (Fantasia)	idem	VI	29	78	713
					Anh.76
idem (Fragment)	idem	V	(With Chorale)	112	753
Jesus Christus, unser Heiland (OB 28)	Christ Jesus our Redeemer	V	32	34	626
*idem (E 15)	idem	VI	31	87	665
idem (CU 20)	idem	VI	30	82	688
idem (Fuga) (CU 21)	idem	VI	33	92	689
idem (E 16)	idem	VI	32	90	666
Jesus, meine Zuversicht	Jesus Christ, my Confidence	V-Anh.	3	103	728

German		English	Vol.	Number	Page	BWV
Komm', Gott Schöp-		Come, God Creator,				
fer, heiliger Geist	(E 17)	Holy Spirit	VII	35	2	667
*idem	(OB 33)	idem	VII	35 Var. B	86	631
*Komm', heil'ger		Come, Lord God, the				
Geist, Herre Gott	(E 1)	Holy Spirit	VII	36	4	651
*idem	(E 2)	idem	VII	37	10	652
Kommst du nun,						
Jesu, vom Himmel		Come Thou now Jesu				
herunter auf Erden ?	(Sch 6)	from Heaven to Earth ?	VII	38	16	650
Kyrie, Gott heiliger		Have mercy on us,				
Geist	(CU 3)	Holy Spirit	VII	39 (c)	23	671
idem	(CU 6)	idem	VII	40 (c)	28	674
Kyrie, Gott Vater in		Have mercy, God,				
Ewigkeit	(CU 1)	Eternal Father	VII	39 (a)	18	669
idem	(CU 4)	idem	VII	40 (a)	26	672
Liebster Jesu, wir		Dearest Jesus we are	V	36	39	706
sind hier		here		(With Chorale)		
*idem	(OB 35)	idem	V	37	40	633
idem		idem	V-Anh.	4	105	730
idem		idem	V-Anh.	5	105	731
idem		idem	IX	12v (b)		754
Lob sei dem		Praise we give to God				
allmächtigen Gott	(OB 4)	Almighty	V	38	40	602
idem (Fughetta)		idem	V	39	41	704
Lobt Gott, ihr		Praise the Lord, all				
Christen, allzugleich	(OB 11)	Christian Men	V	40	42	609
idem		idem	V-Anh.	6	106	732
Meine Seele erhebt		My Soul doth magnify				
den Herren	(Sch 4)	the Lord	VII	42	33	648
idem Fuga sopra il		idem	VII	41	29	733
Magnificat						
Mit Fried' und Freud'		With Peace and Joy I				
ich fahr' dahin	(OB 18)	now depart	V	41	42	616
Nun danket alle Gott	(E 7)	Now thank we all our				
		God	VII	43	34	657
*Nun freut euch, lieben		Now rejoice ye, beloved				
Christen g'mein or		Christian Folk or				
Es ist gewisslich		The Time has surely				
an der Zeit		come	VII	44	36	734
Nun freut euch,		Now rejoice ye, beloved		⎰12xvi (b)		755
lieben Christen		Christian Folk	IX	⎱20 (c)		
g'mein						
Nun komm', der		Come, Thou Saviour				
Heiden Heiland	(OB 1)	of the Gentiles	V	42	44	599
idem (Fughetta)		idem	V	43	45	699
*idem	(E 9)	idem	VII	45	38	659
*idem	(E 10)	idem	VII	46	40	660
*idem	(E 11)	idem	VII	47	42	661
O Gott, du frommer		O God, Thou faithful				
Gott (Partita)		God	V-2	2	68	767
O Herre Gott, dein		O Lord God, Thy				
göttlich's Wort		holy Word	IX	12xiii (b)		757
O Lamm Gottes,		O guiltless Lamb of				
unschuldig	(OB 20)	God	V	44	46	618
*idem	(E 6)	idem	VII	48	45	656
O Mensch bewein'		Mankind bewail thine				
dein' Sünde gross	(OB 24)	awful Sin	V	45	48	622
Puer natus in		A Boy in Bethlehem				
Bethlehem	(OB 5)	is born	V	46	50	603
Schmücke dich, o		Adorn thyself, beloved				
liebe Seele	(E 4)	Soul	VII	49	50	654
Sei gegrüsset, Jesu		Be greeted, gracious				
gütig (Partita)		Jesus	V-2	3	76	768
*Valet will ich dir		I bid thee now fare-				
geben (Fantasia)		well	VII	50	53	735
idem		idem	VII	51	56	736

German		English	Vol.	Number	Page	BWV
Vater unser im Him-melreich	(CU 14)	Our Father, Who art in Heaven	VII	52	60	682
*idem	(CU 15)	idem	V	47	51	683
idem	(OB 37)	idem	V	48	52	636
idem		idem	VII	53	66	737
idem		idem	IX	12xvii (b) 21 (c)		762
Vom Himmel hoch, da komm' ich her	(OB 8)	From Heaven above to Earth I come	V	49	53	606
idem		idem	V-Anh.	7	106	738
idem (Fughetta)		idem	VII	54	67	701
idem (Fuga)		idem	VII	55	68	700
idem (Canonic Variations)		idem	V 2	4	92	769
Vom Himmel kam der Engel Schaar	(OB 9)	From heaven came the angel host	V	50	54	607
Von Gott will ich nicht lassen	(E 8)	From God I do not want to part	VII	56	70	658
Vor deinen Thron tret' ich hiemit (or Wenn wir in hoch-sten Nöthen sein	(E 18)	Now before Thy throne I come (or When we are in deepest need)	VII	58	74	668
idem	(OB 42)	idem	V	51	55	641
Wachet auf, ruft uns die Stimme	(Sch 1)	Awake, the watchman cries	VII	57	72	645
Wenn wir in höchsten Nöthen sein (or Vor deinen Thron tret' ich hiemit)	(OB 42)	When we are in deepest need (or Now before Thy Throne I come)	V	51	55	641
idem	(E 18)	idem	VII	58	74	668
Wer nur den lieben Gott lässt walten	(OB 43)	If thou wilt but accept God's guidance	V	54	57	642
*idem		idem	V	52	56	691
idem	(Sch 3)	idem	VII	59	76	647
idem		idem	V	53 (With Chorale)	56	690
Wie schön leuchtet der Morgenstern		How brightly shines the Morning Star	IX	22(c)		739
idem		idem	IX	12iv (b)		763
Wir Christenleut' hab'n jetzund Freud		We Christians may rejoice to-day	IX	9ix (a) 12x (b) 23 (c)		710
idem	(OB 14)	idem	V	55	58	612
Wir danken dir, Herr Jesu Christ	(OB 25)	Our thanks to Thee, Lord Jesus Christ	V	56	59	623
Wir glauben all' an einen Gott, Schöpfer		We all believe in God, Creator	IX	9iv (a) 12vi (b) 24 (c)		765
idem (Giant Fugue) or the Credo	(CU 12)	idem	VII	60	78	680
idem (Fughetta)	(CU 13)	idem	VII	61	81	681
Wir glauben all an einen Gott, Vater		We all believe in God the Father	VII	62	82	740
Wo soll ich fliehen hin	(Sch 2)	Whither shall I flee?	VII	63	84	646
idem		idem	IX	9viii (a) 12ix (b) 25 (c)		694

*: Variant also included.
CU: Contained in Clavieruebung, Part III (also collected in one volume, P.E. No. 3948).
 E: Contained in " Eighteen Chorales " (also collected into one Volume together with the " Schuebler Chorales," P.E. No. 3947).
OB: Contained in " Orgelbuechlein " (also collected into one Volume, P.E. No. 3946).
Sch.: Contained in " Schuebler Chorales " (also collected into one Volume, together with the " Eighteen Chorales," P.E. No. 3947).

III. BACH ORGAN WORKS

in the order of the nine Volumes of the Peters Urtext Edition

The Nine Volumes (including the Supplement)
Vols. I-VIII (P.E. 240-247), Vol. IX (P.E. 248 or 2067)
References (in parentheses) refer to previous editions

Title	Vol.	No.	Page No.	BWV
6 Sonatas	I	1	2	525-30
Passacaglia & Fugue, C minor	I	7	75	582
Pastorale, F major	I	8	86	590
Prelude and Fugue, C major (*Weimar*)	II	1	2	545
[Variant	II		(iii or) 88	545a]
Prelude and Fugue, G major (*Great*) ..	II	2	7	541
Prelude and Fugue, A major	II	3	14	536
[Variant	II		(iv or) 89	—]
Fantasia and Fugue, G minor (*Great*) ..	II	4	20	542
[Variant	II		(viii or) 93	—]
Prelude and Fugue, F minor	II	5	29	534
— C minor	II	6	36	546
— C major (*Leipzig*)	II	7	46	547
— A minor (*Great*)	II	8	54	543
— E minor (*Wedge* or *Scissors*) ..	II	9	64	548
— B minor (*Great* or *Sands of Time*) ..	II	10	78	544
Prelude and Fugue, E flat major				
(*St. Anne* or *Trinity*)	III	1	1	552
Toccata and Fugue, F major (*Colossal*				
or *Tremendous*)	III	2	16	540
— D minor (*Dorian*)	III	3	30	538
Prelude and Fugue, D minor (*Fiddle*) ..	III	4	42	539
— G minor	III	5	48	535
Fantasia and Fugue, C minor (*Great*) ..	III	6	55	537
Toccata (*or Prelude*) and Fugue, C major	III	7	62	566
[Variant, E major	III		(vii or) 94	—]
Toccata, Adagio and Fugue, C major ..	III	8	72	564
Prelude and Fugue, A minor	III	9	84	551
— E minor (*Short, Cathedral, Night-*				
watchman)	III	10	88	533
Prelude and Fugue, C major (*Trumpet*) ..	IV	1	2	531
— G major	IV	2	8	550
— D major	IV	3	14	532
[Variant	IV		(v or) 79	532a]
Toccata and Fugue, D minor	IV	4	24	565
Prelude and Fugue, C minor (*Arnstadt*) ..	IV	5	32	549
Fugue, C minor (*Legrenzi* or *Double*				
Fugue)	IV	6	36	574
— G minor (*Little* or *Folk Song*) ..	IV	7	42	578
— B minor (*Corelli*)	IV	8	46	579
— C minor (*C.P.E. Bach?*)	IV	9	50	575
Canzona, D minor	IV	10	54	588

Title				Vol.	No.	Page No.	BWV
Fantasia, G major	..	..	..	IV	11	58	572
— C minor	..	..	..	IV	12	66	562
						(Fant. only)	
Prelude, A minor ..	..	..	..	IV	13	68	569
Trio, D minor	..	..	..	IV	14	72	583

56 Shorter Chorale Preludes:

Title		Vol.	No.	Page No.	BWV
Ach wie nichtig (OB 45) ..	..	V	1	2	644
Alle Menschen müssen sterben (OB 44) ..		V	2	2	643
Christe, du Lamm Gottes (OB 21)	..	V	3	3	619
Christ ist erstanden (OB 29)	..	V	4	4	627
Christ lag in Todesbanden (OB 27)	..	V	5	7	625
Christum wir sollen loben schon (OB 13)	V	6	8	611	
idem, or, Was fürcht'st du (Fughetta)	..	V	7	9	696
Christus, der uns selig macht (OB 22) ..		V	8	10	620
[Variant ..	..	V		(iii or) 108	620a]
Da Jesus an dem Kreuze stund (OB 23) ..		V	9	11	621
Das alte Jahr vergangen ist (OB 16)	..	V	10	12	614
Der Tag, der ist so freudenreich (OB 7)..		V	11	13	605
Dies sind die heil'gen zehn Gebot' (OB 36)	V	12	14	635	
Durch Adams Fall ist ganz verderbt (OB 38) ..	..	V	13	15	637
Erstanden ist der heil'ge Christ (OB 30)	V	14	16	628	
Erschienen ist der herrliche Tag (OB 31)	V	15	17	629	
Es ist das Heil uns kommen her (OB 39)..		V	16	18	638
Gelobet seist du, Jesu Christ (OB 6)	..	V	17	19	604
idem (Fughetta)	..	V	18	20	697
Gott, durch deine Güte; or, Gottes Sohn ist kommen (OB 2)	..	V	19	20	600
Gottes Sohn ist kommen (Fughetta)	..	V	20	22	703
Helft mir Gottes Güte preisen (OB 15) ..		V	21	23	613
Herr Christ, der ein'ge Gottes Sohn: or, Herr Gott, nun sei gepreiset (OB 3) ..		V	22	24	601
Herr Christ, der ein'ge Gottes Sohn (Fughetta)	..	V	23	25	698
Herr Gott, nun schleuss den Himmel auf (OB 19) ..	..	V	24	26	617
Herr Jesu Christ, dich zu uns wend' (OB 34) ..	..	V	25	28	632
Herr Jesu Christ, dich zu uns wend'	..	V	26	28	709
Herzlich thut mich verlangen	..	V	27	30	727
Heut' triumphieret Gottes Sohn (OB 32)		V	28	30	630
Hilf, Gott, dass mir's gelinge (OB 26)..		V	29	32	624
Ich ruf' zu dir, Herr Jesu Christ (OB 40)..		V	30	33	639
Jesu, meine Freude (OB 12)	..	V	31	34	610
Jesus Christus, unser Heiland (OB 28)..		V	32	34	626
In dich hab' ich gehoffet, Herr (OB 41)..		V	33	35	640
In dir ist Freude (OB 17)	..	V	34	36	615
In dulci jubilo (OB 10) ..	..	V	35	38	608
Liebster Jesu, wir sind hier	..	V	36	39	706
Liebster Jesu, wir sind hier (OB 35)	..	V	37	40	633
[Variant ..	..	V		(iv or) 109	634]
Lob sei dem allmächtigen Gott (OB 4)..		V	38	40	602
Lob sei dem allmächtigen Gott (Fughetta)	V	39	41	704	

Title	Vol.	No.	Page No.	BWV
Lobt Gott, ihr Christen, allzugleich (OB 11)	V	40	42	609
Mit Fried' und Freud' ich fahr' dahin (OB 18)	V	41	42	616
Nun komm' der Heiden Heiland (OB 1)..	V	42	44	599
Nun komm' der Heiden Heiland (Fughetta)	V	43	45	699
O Lamm Gottes unschuldig (OB 20) ..	V	44	46	618
O Mensch, bewein dein' Sünde gross (OB 24)	V	45	48	622
Puer natus in Bethlehem (OB 5) ..	V	46	50	603
Vater unser im Himmelreich (CU 15) ..	V	47	51	683
[Variant	V		(iv or) 109	683a]
Vater unser im Himmelreich (OB 37) ..	V	48	52	636
Vom Himmel hoch, da komm' ich her (OB 8)	V	49	53	606
Vom Himmel kam der Engel Schaar (OB 9)	V	50	54	607
Wenn wir in höchsten Nöthen sein (OB 42)	V	51	55	641
Wer nur den lieben Gott lässt walten ..	V	52	56	691
[Variant	V		(vi or) 111	691a]
Wer nur den lieben Gott lässt walten ..	V	53	56	690
idem (OB 43)	V	54	57	642
Wir Christenleut' (OB 14)	V	55	58	612
Wir danken dir, Herr Jesu Christ (OB 25)	V	56	59	623

Chorale-Variations

Title	Vol.	No.	Page No.	BWV
Christ, der du bist der helle Tag ..	V-2	1	60	766
O Gott, du frommer Gott	V-2	2	68	767
Sei gegrüsset, Jesu gütig	V-2	3	76	768
Vom Himmel hoch . . . (Kanonische Veränderungen)	V-2	4	92	769

Chorale Preludes (Anhang)

Title	Vol.	No.	Page No.	BWV
Gelobet seist du, Jesu Christ	V-Anh.	1	102	722
In dulci jubilo	V-Anh.	2	103	729
Jesus, meine Zuversicht	V-Anh.	3	103	728
Liebster Jesu, wir sind hier	V-Anh.	4	105	730
idem	V-Anh.	5	105	731
Lobt Gott, ihr Christen, allzugleich ..	V-Anh.	6	106	732
Vom Himmel hoch da komm' ich her ..	V-Anh.	7	106	738
Jesu meine Freude (fragment)	V		(vii or) 112	753

Longer Chorale Preludes

Title	Vol.	No.	Page No.	BWV
Ach Gott und Herr (also attrib. Walther)	VI	1	3	693
Ach bleib bei uns, Herr Jesu Christ (Sch. 5)	VI	2	4	649
Allein Gott in der Höh' sei Ehr' ..	VI	3	6	711
idem	VI	4	8	717
idem (CU 7)	VI	5	10	675
idem (CU 8)	VI	6	12	676
[Variant	VI		(Anh. 2, or) 96	676a]
idem (Trio) (E 14)..	VI	7	17	664
[Variant	VI		(Anh. 3, or), 97	664a]

Title	Vol.	No.	Page No.	BWV
idem (E 13)	VI	8	22	663
[Variant	VI	(Anh. 6, or) 100		663a]
idem (E 12)	VI	9	26	662
idem (CU 9) Fughetta	VI	10	29	677
idem Fuga	VI	11	30	716
An Wasserflüssen Babylon	VI	12a	32	653b
idem (E 3)	VI	12b	34	653
[Variant	VI	(Anh. 9, or) 103		653a]
Aus tiefer Noth . . . (CU 18)	VI	13	36	686
idem (CU 19)	VI	14	38	687
Christ lag in Todesbanden	VI	15	40	718
idem (Fantasia)	VI	16	43	695
[Variant	VI	(Anh. 10, or) 104		695a]
Christ unser Herr zum Jordan kam (CU 16)	VI	17	46	684
idem (CU 17)	VI	18	49	685
Dies sind die heil'gen zehn Gebot' (CU 10)	VI	19	50	678
idem (Fughetta) (CU 11)	VI	20	54	679
Durch Adams Fall . . . (Fuga)	VI	21	56	705
Ein' feste Burg ist unser Gott	VI	22	58	720
Gelobet seist du, Jesu Christ	VI	23	61	723
Gott der Vater wohn' uns bei	VI	24	62	748
[Variant	VI	(Anh. 12, or) 106		748a]
Gottes Sohn ist kommen	VI	25	64	724
Herr Gott, dich loben wir	VI	26	65	725
Herr Jesu Christ, dich zu uns wend' (E 5)	VI	27	70	655
[Variants	VI	(Anh. 13, 14, or) 107, 108		655a-c]
Ich hab' mein' Sach' Gott heimgestellt	VI	28	74	707
Jesu, meine Freude (Fantasia)	VI	29	78	713
[Variant	VI	(Anh. 16, or) 110		713a]
Jesus Christus, unser Heiland (CU 20)	VI	30	82	688
idem (E 15)	VI	31	87	665
[Variant	VI	(Anh. 18, or) 112		665a]
idem (E 16)	VI	32	90	666
idem (Fuga) (CU 21)	VI	33	92	689
In dich hab' ich gehoffet, Herr (Fughetta)	VI	34	94	712
Komm, Gott, Schöpfer, heiliger Geist (E 17)	VII	35	2	667
[Variants (including OB 33)	VII	(Anh. 2, or) 86		631,a]
Komm, heil'ger Geist, Herre Gott (E 1)	VII	36	4	651
idem (E 2)	VII	37	10	652
[Variants to E 1 and 2:	VII	(Anh. 2, 4 or) 86, 88		651a, 652a
Kommst du nun, Jesu . . . (Sch. 6)	VII	38	16	650
Kyrie, Gott Vater in Ewigkeit (CU 1)	VII	39a	18	669
Christe, aller Welt Trost (CU 2)	VII	39b	20	670
Kyrie, Gott heiliger Geist (CU 3)	VII	39c	23	671
Kyrie, Gott Vater in Ewigkeit (CU 4)	VII	40a	26	672
Christe, aller Welt Trost (CU 5)	VII	40b	27	673
Kyrie, Gott heiliger Geist (CU 6)	VII	40c	28	674
Meine Seele erhebt den Herren (Fuga sopra il Magnificat)	VII	41	29	733
Meine Seele erhebt den Herren (Sch. 4)	VII	42	33	648

Title	Vol.	No.	Page No.	BWV
Nun danket alle Gott (E 7)	VII	43	34	657
Nun freut euch, lieben Christen g'mein or,				
Es ist gewisslich an der Zeit	VII	44	36	734
[Variant	VII	(Anh. 7, or)	91	734a]
Nun komm', der Heiden Heiland (E 9)	VII	45	38	659
[Variant	VII	(Anh. 8, or)	92	659a]
Nun komm', der Heiden Heiland (E 10)..	VII	46	40	660
[Variants	VII (Anh. 9, 10, or)		93, 94	660a, b]
Nun komm', der Heiden Heiland (E 11)..	VII	47	42	661
[Variant	VII	(Anh. 12, or)	96	661a]
O Lamm Gottes unschuldig (E 6) ..	VII	48	45	656
[Variant	VII	(Anh. 13, or)	97	656a]
Schmücke dich, o liebe Seele (E 4) ..	VII	49	50	654
Valet will ich dir geben (Fantasia) ..	VII	50	53	735
[Variant	VII	(Anh. 16, or)	100	735a]
Valet will ich dir geben	VII	51	56	736
Vater unser im Himmelreich (CU 14) ..	VII	52	60	682
idem	VII	53	66	737
Vom Himmel hoch . . . (Fughetta) ..	VII	54	67	701
idem (Fuga)	VII	55	68	700
Von Gott will ich nicht lassen (E 8) ..	VII	56	70	658
[Variant	VII	(Anh. 18, or)	102	658a]
Wachet auf, ruft uns die Stimme (Sch. 1)	VII	57	72	645
Wenn wir in höchsten Nöthen sein (E 18);				
or, Vor deinen Thron tret'ich hiemit ..	VII	58	74	668
Wer nur den lieben Gott lässt walten				
(Sch. 3)	VII	59	76	647
Wir glauben all an einen Gott, Schöpfer				
(CU 12) (Credo or Giant Fugue) ..	VII	60	78	680
idem (Fughetta) (CU 13)	VII	61	81	681
Wir glauben all an einen Gott, Vater ..	VII	62	82	740
Wo soll ich fliehen hin (Sch. 2); or, Auf				
meinen lieben Gott	VII	63	84	646

Miscellaneous Compositions:

Concertos (4) after Vivaldi and others ..	VIII	1-4	2	592-5
8 Short Preludes and Fugues	VIII	5	48	553-560
Allabreve, D major	VIII	6	72	589
Prelude, C major (manuals only) ..	VIII	7	76	943
Prelude, C major (doubtful)	VIII	8	77	567
Fantasia, C major (Andreas Bach Book)	VIII	9	78	570
Fugue, C major (Hexachord)	VIII	10	80	946
Prelude, G major	VIII	11	82	568
Fugue, G minor (from Cantata 131) ..	VIII	12	85	131a

Volume IX—a, b and c refer to the three different editions of this volume:

a   to the F. A. Roitzsch edition (the first) of 1881,
b   to the M. Seiffert revision of 1904,
c   to the (current) edition of H. Keller (1940/50).

The page references have been omitted to save complication.
In a & b, the Chorale Preludes were numbered as a set, 9 & 12 respectively, and the individual Preludes had subsidiary numbers as shown. In c each Prelude was numbered individually.

Title	a	b	c	BWV
Fantasia and Fugue, A minor	1	1	6	561
Fantasia, B minor, *con imitazione* ..	—	—	1 (not in a, b)	563
Fugue, G major	2	2	7	576
Fugue, G major, *à la Gigue*	4	4	2	577
Fugue, D major	5	5	— (not in c)	580
Fantasia, G (doubtful) (*Concerto*) ..	6	6	4	571
Kleines harmonisches Labyrinth, C major	3	3	9	591
Concerto, E flat major, *Vivaldi*	—	7	— (not in a, c)	597
Trio, G major, from Gamba Sonata No. 1	—	8	3 (not in a)	1027a
Trio, G major (by Telemann)	—	10	8 (not in a)	586
Trio, C minor (by Krebs?)	7	9	10	585
Aria, F major (after Couperin)	8	11	5	587
Pedal-Exercitium, G minor	—	—	11 (not in a, b)	598

Chorale Preludes:

Title	a	b	c	BWV
Ach Gott und Herr (attrib. Walther) ..	9-i	—	— (not in b, c)	692
idem	9-ii	12-i	12	714
Ach Gott vom Himmel	9-vi	12-vii	13	741
Ach Herr, mich armen Sünder	—	12-xiv	— (not in a, c)	742
Ach was ist doch unser Leben	—	12-xv	— (not in a, c)	743
Ach was soll ich Sünder machen (Partita)	—	—	26 (not in a, b)	770
Allein Gott in der Höh	—	—	14 (not in a, b)	715
Auf meinen lieben Gott	9-iii	12-ii	15	744
Aus der Tiefe rufe ich	9-x	12-xi	16	745
Christ lag in Todesbanden (by Pachelbel)	9-xi	—	— (not in b, c)	Anh.171
Christus, der uns selig macht	—	12-xviii	— (not in a, c)	747
Das Jesulein soll doch mein Trost ..	9-vii	12-viii	17	702
Herr Jesu Christ, dich zu uns wend' ..	—	—	18 (not in a, b)	726
In dulci jubilo	—	12-xii	19 (not in a)	751
Jesu Leiden, Pein und Tod (by J. C. Vogler)	9-v	—	— (not in b, c)	Anh.57
Jesu, der du meine Seele	—	12-iii	— (not in a, c)	752
Liebster Jesu, wir sind hier	—	12-v	— (not in a, c)	754
Nun freut euch, lieben Christen, g'mein..	—	12-xvi	20 (not in a)	755
O Herre Gott, dein göttlich's Wort ..	—	12-xiii	— (not in a, c)	757
Vater unser im Himmelreich	—	12-xvii	21 (not in a)	762
Wie schön leuchtet der ⎱ .. .. Morgenstern ⎰	— ⎰	⎱ 12-iv ⎰ — ⎰	— (not in a, c) 22 (not in a, b)	763 739
Wir Christenleut' hab'n jetzund Freud'..	9-ix	12-x	23	710
Wir glauben all an einen Gott, Schöpfer..	9-iv	12-vi	24	765
Wo soll ich fliehen hin	9-viii	12-ix	25	694

IV. NICKNAMED ORGAN COMPOSITIONS
compiled by Max Hinrichsen

The nicknames invented in England and America during the last hundred years to assist in distinguishing similar organ works in identical keys, etc., are listed alphabetically below, together with their Schmieder BWV Numbers. These nicknames are also quoted in the original introductions to the individual volumes of the Peters Urtext Edition reprinted in Hinrichsen's Eighth Music Book, which contains descriptions of each individual composition. The Roman figures after the BWV Numbers refer to the relevant volume of the basic edition of Bach Organ Works (Peters Edition).

BWV 577   IX   **A la Gigue** or **Jig.** Fugue in G major. Not so named by the composer, apparently, though the description is correct enough. Probably composed for a two-manual and pedal harpsichord (*Scholes*). Jig is an old dance in binary form in some kind of animated triple time, usually 6-8 or 12-8; in Italian giga and in French gigue. It is one of the dances regularly found in Suites, where it forms the finale (*Blom*).

BWV 549   IV   **Arnstadt.** Prelude and Fugue in C minor.

BWV 533   III   **Cathedral,** or **Short** or **Nightwatchman.** Prelude and Fugue in E minor.

BWV 540   III   **Colossal** (*Parry*) or **Tremendous** (*Mendelssohn*) Toccata (or Prelude) and Fugue in F major.

BWV 571   IX   **Concerto.** Fantasia in G major.

BWV 563   IX   **Con imitazione.** Fantasia in B minor.

BWV 579   IV   **Corelli.** Fugue in B minor on a theme of Corelli, Op. 3 No. 4.

BWV 680   VII   **Credo (The)** or **Giant.** Fugue in D minor, from Clavierue-bung, Part III. (We all believe in God, Creator). Giant is merely a nickname due to the stalking figure in the pedal (*Scholes*).

BWV 538   III   **Dorian.** Toccata and Fugue in D minor. In the Dorian mode the scale is represented by the white keys beginning on the note D.

BWV 574   IV   **Double** or **Legrenzi.** Fugue in C minor. Many manuscript copies, as the Foreword to the first edition explains, bear the additional designation "Thema Legrenzianium elaboratum cum subjecto pedaliter ab J. S. Bach". It is therefore likely that the theme is by Giovanni Legrenzi (1626-1690). Legrenzi was an Italian composer, organist and chapel master, who died at Venice where he had lived many years.

BWV 539   III   **Fiddle.** Prelude [manuals only] and Fugue in D minor. The Fugue is a transcription by Bach of the Fugue from his Sonata in G minor for Solo Violin transposed into D minor.

BWV 578   IV   **Folk Song** or **Little.** Fugue in G minor.

BWV 680   VII   **Giant** or **The Credo.** Fugue in D minor. See above under Credo.

BWV 537   III   **Great.** Prelude (or Fantasia) and Fugue in C minor.

BWV 541   II   **Great.** Prelude and Fugue in G major.

BWV 542	II	**Great.** Prelude (or Fantasia) and Fugue in G minor.
BWV 543	II	**Great.** Prelude and Fugue in A minor.
BWV 544	II	**Great or The Sands of Time** (*Samuel Wesley*). Prelude and Fugue in B minor.

BWV 946   VIII   **Hexachord.** Fugue in C major. As *Eric Blom* says in 'Everyman's Dictionary of Music', a Hexachord (from the Greek=six sounds) is a system of dividing the musical scale into groups of 6 notes, which *Guido d'Arezzo* in the 11th century named Ut, Re, Mi, Fa, Sol, La. They could begin on 3 different notes, the lowest starting from G on the bottom line of the bass clef, then marked with the Greek letter Γ (Gamma), the other two being C and F above; and these were repeated 4 times, starting on G, C, F and F counting upwards.

The remaining notes were named by letters from A to G, as to-day, but the syllables remained the same in each hexachord, so that in the first G was Ut, A was Re, etc.; in the 2nd C became Ut, D Re, etc.; in the 3rd F became Ut, G Re, etc.; and so on throughout the 7 hexachords. But each hexachord had to have its only semitone interval between the notes marked with the syllables Mi and Fa, so that in the 3rd and 6th the 4th note, which fell on B, had to be flattened.

Thus the 1st accidental was introduced into the diatonic scale, and it was through this that the modes began to give way to the modern major and minor scales. Up to the time of *Purcell* the hexachordal system persisted in so far as the syllables of the Gamut (a word derived from 'Gamma Ut') pertaining to it remained in use. Pieces are found described as being, for example, in 'C fa ut' (sometimes spelt 'C faut').

Fantasy is a type of composition cultivated by the English virginalists, a piece of the Fantasy or Fancy species based on the 1st 6 notes of the scale, ascending or descending. The pieces were often entitled 'Ut, re, mi, fa, sol, la'.

BWV 577	IX	**Jig or à la Gigue.** Fugue in G major. See under 'A la Gigue', above.
BWV 574	IV	**Legrenzi or Double Fugue** in C minor. See above under Double.
BWV 547	II	**Leipzig.** Prelude and Fugue in C major.
BWV 578	IV	**Little or Folk Song.** Fugue in G minor.
BWV 733	VII	**Magnificat (On the).** A Fugue on "Meine Seele erhebt den Herren" (My soul doth magnify the Lord).
BWV 533	III	**Nightwatchman, or Cathedral, or Short.** Prelude and Fugue in E minor.
BWV 590	I	**Pastorale in F.**
BWV 248	P-38	**Pastorale.** Sinfonia to Part II of the Christmas Oratorio, arr. for the Organ by Henry G. Ley.
BWV 878	H-1c	**Saints in Glory (The)** (*Samuel Wesley*). Fugue in E major. Well-tempered Klavier, Vol. II No. 9, arranged for the Organ by Francis G. Walker.
BWV 544	II	**Sands of Time (The)** (*Samuel Wesley*), **or Great.** Prelude and Fugue in B minor.

| BWV 645/50 P-3947 | **Schübler Chorales.** 6 Chorales, named after the publisher of the work. |
| BWV 552 | III | **St. Anne** or **Trinity.** Prelude and Fugue in E flat major. The title has been given by some English writer, or has grown up amongst British organists, from the chance that the first subject is the same as the first line of *Croft's* hymn-tune St. Anne (first published 1708) which itself was so called because Croft was organist of St. Anne's Church, Soho, London.
The same phrase is found in two movements of *Handel's* Chandos Anthem, 'O Praise the Lord with one consent'. *Harvey Grace* in 'The Organ Works of Bach' (1922), points out that but for the first two notes changing places the phrase is also the first line of the Chorale 'Was mein Gott will'; and it may be that in some variants these notes are in the same order as in the fugue subject, so that the fugue may be, in effect, a sort of Chorale Prelude.
The Prelude to the St. Anne's Fugue has no association with it in the original publication (the Clavieruebung). Thus we find *Mendelssohn* writing to his mother from England: "Ask Fanny" (his sister) "what she thinks of my intention of playing Bach's Organ Prelude in E flat major together with the Fugue at the end of the same book. I suppose she will disapprove of this, yet I think I am right". (*P. A. Scholes*). |

BWV 548	II	**Scissors** or **Wedge.** Prelude and Fugue in E minor. See under Wedge below.
BWV 533	III	**Short,** or **Cathedral** or **Nightwatchman.** Prelude and Fugue in E minor.
BWV 586	IX	**Telemann Trio** in G major.
BWV 540	III	**Tremendous** (*Mendelssohn*) or **Colossal** (*Parry*) Toccata (or Prelude) and Fugue in F major.
BWV 552	III	**Trinity** or **St. Anne.** Prelude and Fugue in E flat major. See under St. Anne above.
BWV 531	IV	**Trumpet.** Prelude and Fugue in C.
BWV 593	VIII	**Vivaldi.** Concerto in A minor, after Vivaldi Op. 3 No. 8.
BWV 596 P-3002		**Vivaldi.** Concerto in D minor, after Vivaldi's "L'Estro Armonico", Concerto Grosso Op. 3 No. 11. This was previously attributed to W. F. Bach.
BWV 594	VIII	**Vivaldi.** Concerto in C major on a theme of Vivaldi Op. 7 No. 11.
BWV 597	IX(b)	**Vivaldi.** Concerto in E flat major, on a theme of Vivaldi, previously attributed to W. F. Bach.
BWV 548	II	**Wedge** or **Scissors.** Prelude and Fugue in E minor. Merely a nickname due to the melodic shape of the subject, which, beginning by alternating notes (in a rocking style) a minor third apart, expands its alternations step by step (*P. A. Scholes*).
BWV 545	II	**Weimar.** Prelude and Fugue in C major.

V. SUGGESTED METRONOME INDICATIONS

for Volume One (Hermann Keller, 1948):

Trio Sonatas Nos. 1 to 6:

1. BWV 525. E flat ♩=76, ♪=92, ♩=100 (12 mins.)
2. BWV 526. C m. — ♪=84, ♩=92 (10 mins.)
3. BWV 527. D m. ♩=63, ♪=69, ♪=132 (12 mins.)
4. BWV 528. E m. ♪=70, ♩=96, ♪=84, ♪=108 (11½ mins.)
5. BWV 529. C ♩=92 to 96, ♪=66, ♩=96 to 104 (14 mins
6. BWV 530. G ♩=104, ♪=63, ♩=88 (11 mins.)

for Volume Two (F. K. Griepenkerl, 1844):

1. BWV 545.	Prelude	♩=54	Fugue		♩=108
2. BWV 541.	,,	♩=69	,,		♩=76
3. BWV 536.	,,	♩=66	,,		♩=104
4. BWV 542.	Fantasia	♪=84	,,		♩=69
5. BWV 534.	Prelude	♩=50	,,		♩=112
6. BWV 546.	,,	♩=66	,,		♩=92
7. BWV 547.	,,	♪=126	,,		♩=60
8. BWV 543.	,,	♩=60	,,		♪=120
9. BWV 548.	,,	♩=60	,,		♩=108
10. BWV 544.	,,	♪=80	,,		♩=66

for Volume Four (F. K. Griepenkerl, 1845):

1. BWV 531. Prelude ♩=63 Fuga ♩=66 in C (Trumpet)
2. BWV 550. Prelude ♩=60 .... in G
   Grave ♩=54 Fuga ♩=104 in G
3. BWV 532. Prelude ♩=60 .... in D
   Alla breve ♩=60 .... in D
   Adagio ♩=54 Fuga ♩=80 in D
4. BWV 565. Toccata ——— Fuga ♩=72 in D m.
5. BWV 549. Prelude ♩=58 Fuga ♩=63 in C m. (Arnstadt)
6. BWV 574. Fugue ♩=80 .... in C m. (Legrenzi)
7. BWV 578. Fugue ♩=76 .... in G m. (Little or Folksong)
8. BWV 579. Fugue ♩=80 .... in B m. (Corelli)
9. BWV 575. Fugue ♩=72 .... in C m.
10. BWV 588. Canzona C ♩=84 $\frac{3}{2}$♩=72 ...... in D m.
11. BWV 572. Fantasia $\frac{12}{8}$ ♩.=66 C ♩=60 C ♪=72..in G
12. BWV 562. Fantasia ♩=60 .... in C m.
13. BWV 569. Prelude ♩=66 .... in A m.
14. BWV 583. Trio ♪=76 .... in D m.

BIBLIOGRAPHY

(a) Books:

Adlung, Jacob. *Musica Mechanica Organoedi.* Berlin, 1768.

David, H. T. and Arthur Mendel (Editors and Translators). *The Bach Reader.* New York, 1947.

Donington, Robert. *Tempo and Rhythm in Bach's Organ Music.* London, 1960.

Flade, E. *Der Orgelbauer Gottfried Silbermann.* Leipzig, 1953.

Frotscher, Gotthold. *Geschichte des Orgelspiels und der Orgel Komposition.* 2 Vols. Berlin, 1935 and 1959 (for British Commonwealth, U.S.A. and Canada: Peters Edition).

Keller, Hermann. *Die Orgelwerke Bachs.* Leipzig, 1948 (now Peters Edition, London and N.Y.).

Klotz, H. *Über die Orgelkunst der Gotik, der Renaissance und des Barock.* Kassel, 1934.

Mahrenholz, Christian. *Die Orgelregister, ihre Geschichte und ihr Bau.* Kassel, 1930.

Schweitzer, Albert. *J. S. Bach.* London, 1930.

Spitta, Phillip. *J. S. Bach.* London and N.Y., 1951.

Sumner, William L. *Arp Schnitger.* Organ Institute Quarterly, Andover, Mass., 1955-6.

[Sumner, William L. *Bach's Organ Registration* (and related matters). London, 1961].

Sumner, William L. *The Organ of Bach.* With a detailed Bibliography and a large number of Articles relating to Bach's Organ Music. *Hinrichsen's Eighth Music Book.* London, 1956.

Taylor, Stainton de B. *The Chorale Preludes of J. S. Bach.* Oxford, 1941.

(b) Music:

Bach, Johann Sebastian. *The Complete Organ Works of Bach in 9 Volumes.* P.E. Nos. 240-247, 2067.

Buxtehude, Dietrich. *Organ Works.*
- Vol. I: The large-scale Organ Works: 9 Preludes and Fugues; Toccata and Fugue; Fugue C; Passacaglia in 4 Sections, each with 7 Vars.; Chaconne E m., 21 contrasting Vars., some of them very expressive and moving; Canzonetta G, a short fugato piece, reminding us of Frescobaldi or Pachelbel. P.E. No. 4449.
- Vol. II: The 24 Chorale Preludes. P.E. No. 4457.

Chorale Preludes of the 17th and 18th Centuries (Hermann Keller). P. E. No. 4448.

INDEX

APPENDIX

BACH'S ORGAN MUSIC

A. THE COMPLETE ORGAN WORKS OF BACH
in nine Volumes

Hermann Keller, in ' The Organ Works of Bach,' gives credit to the authoritative Griepenkerl-Peters Edition of the Bach Organ Works as the first in value. He assigns the Bach Gesellschaft edition second place, since numerous important Manuscript copies, which were available to Griepenkerl, were lost soon afterwards.

1. Passacaglia & Fugue C m.; Pastorale F; 6 Trio Sonatas. (P-240)

2. Fantasia & Fugue G m. (*Great*); 9 Preludes & Fugues: C (*Weimar*), G (*Great*), A. F m., C m. (*Great*), C (*Leipzig*), A m. (*Great*), E m. (*Wedge* or *Scissors*), B m. (*Great*). (P-241)

3. Fantasia & Fugue C m.; 6 Preludes & Fugues: E flat (*St. Anne* or *Trinity*), D m. (*Fiddle Fugue*), G m., C, A m., E m. (*Cathedral, Short,* or *Nightwatchman*); 3 Toccatas and Fugues: F, D m. (*Dorian*), C. (P-242)

4. Canzona D m.; 2 Fantasias: G, C m.; 4 Fugues: C m. (*Legrenzi* or *Double Fugue*), G m. (*Little* or *Folksong*), B m. (*Corelli*), C m.; Praeludium A m.; 4 Preludes & Fugues: C (*Trumpet*), G, D, C m. (*Arnstadt*); Toccata & Fugue D m.; Trio D m. (P-243)

5. 56 Short Chorale Preludes; 5 Canonic Vars. on ' *Vom Himmel hoch* '; 7 Chorale Preludes; Chorale Vars. on ' *Christ, der du bist der helle Tag,*' on ' *O Gott, du frommer Gott,*' on ' *Sei gegruesset Jesu guetig* ' (easy). (P-244)

6. 34 Chorale Preludes (Chorales A to J), incl. ' *Schuebler* ' No. 5; ' 18 *Great Chorales* ' Nos. 3, 5, 12, 13 to 16; *Clavieruebung*, Part III Nos. 7 to 11, 16 to 21. (P-245)

7. Chorale Preludes (Chorales K to Z), incl. No. 60: ' *Wir glauben all' an einen Gott* ' (The Giant Fugue or The Credo); ' *Schuebler* ' Nos. 1 to 4, 6; ' 18 *Great Chorales* ' Nos. 1, 2, 4, 6 to 11, 17, 18; *Clavieruebung* Part III Nos. 1 to 6, 12 to 15. (P-246)

8. Allabreve D; 4 Concerti: G, A m. (*Vivaldi*), C (*Vivaldi*), C; Fantasia C; 2 Fugues: C (*Hexachord*), G m.; 3 Preludes: C, C, G; 8 Short Preludes & Fugues: C, D m., E m., F, G, G m., A m., B flat. (P-247)

9. Aria F; 14 Chorale Preludes; Partita: Chorale Variations on '*Ach, was soll ich Suender machen*'; Fantasia G (5th Concerto); Fantasia con imitazione B m.; Fantasia and Fugue A m.; 2 Fugues: G (*Fugue à la Gigue*), G; A Short Harmonical Labyrinthus C m.; Pedal-Exercitium G m.; 3 Trios: G, G (*Telemann*), C m. (P-2067)

B. THE COMPOSITIONS BASED ON CHORALES
in three Volumes

This new collection follows in every respect the liturgical sequence used by Bach himself and can be regarded as an authoritative edition

1. The Little Organ Book (*Orgelbüchlein*). 45 Chorale Preludes (P-3946)
2. The Six Schuebler Chorales and the eighteen Chorales (P-3947)
3. Clavieruebung, Part III with Catechism Preludes and the four Duettos (P-3948)

C. OTHER BACH CHORALE PRELUDE COLLECTIONS

in five Volumes

1. Chorale Preludes *for Christmas* (P-2067d)..
2. Chorale Preludes (thirty) *in progressive order* (P-2178b)................:..............
3. Chorale Preludes from Clavieruebung, *re-arranged for small hands*, manuals only (H-376)..
   − from the above: Allein Gott; Aus tiefer Noth (H-376a)..........................
4. Chorales extended, from 3 Church Cantatas: Nos. 4, 24, 129: Christ Jesus, only Son of God; O God, Thou God of Faith; Let Heaven and Earth rejoice (H-353) ....
5. Preludes (three) on ' *In dulci jubilo*,' preceded by Bach's choral setting (H-356)

D. MISCELLANEOUS BACH ORGAN WORKS

(a) on two staves:

Album of Original Bach Works. This new collection of 24 pieces on two staves, edited by Hermann Keller, includes only compositions especially suitable for small organ. Entrata F; Menuet and Trio F; Bourrée A; Menuet Eb; Sarabande Bb; Praeludiums: C, G, D m; Andante F; Adagio D m; Vivaldi Organ Concerto A m.; Fugatos: E m., G; Fantasias: C, D m.; Fuga D m.; Andante C; Larghetto C m. and Vivace F *from the Pastorale*; Fuga D m. *from* ' *The Art of Fugue*'; Aria D; Fantasia con imitazione B m ; Praeludium and Fugato E m.; Praeludium et Fuga A m.; Praeludium (Rondo) F m.; Allegro *from Vivaldi Concerto G*; Fantasia con Fuga A m., Aria D (P-4510)................................

Air *on the G String* (D-280)..

Andante *from fifth Flute Sonata.* Organ & Violin (P-3183)..........................

Articulation in Organ-Playing, including a ' Little Organ Book for Manuals only', based on 31 Chorale Preludes and Chorales by Bach in the order of the Liturgical Year (Gordon Phillips). Foreword by R. Donington (H-1001)............

Jesu, Men's Desire (De-728)..

Siciliano *from second Flute Sonata* (De-752)..

Toccata - Fantasia con Fuga in D (P-211a)..

(b) on three staves, in separate form:

Christmas Oratio: Pastoral Symphony (H. G. Ley) (P-38a)..........................

Come, Holy Ghost, Facsimile reproduction of the ' Fantasia super Veni Sancte Spiritus,' with Portrait and Critical Analysis (Wackernagel) (De-117)............

Concerto in D m. after Vivaldi (' *L'Estro Armonico* ') (P-3002)....................

Concerto in A m. after Vivaldi (N-4036)..

Fuga in E, from ' 48 ' (*The Saints in Glory*) (P-1c)....................................

German Organ Mass *Clavieruebung*, Part III (P-3948)................................

Jesu, Men's Desire (P-264)..

Magnificat. The Organ Part of the orchestral accompaniment (P-29b)..................

Passacaglia in C m. (N-4171)..

Ricercar a 6 voci *from Musical Offering* (Hermann Keller) (P-4528)........................

Toccata and Fugue in D m. (P-261)...

(c) on three staves, in volume form:

Album, containing Pastorale in F, Fugue in G à la Gigue, and Fugue in B m. on a theme of Corelli (H-355)..

Art of Fugue. The complete work laid out for the Organ in an eminently practical manner (H. Schuricht) (P-218i/k):
I. Contrapunctus I-XI. II. Contrapunctus XII-XIX and Chorale.......................

Bach's Art of Part-Playing. A collection of six short Trios with advice on registration and method of study (S. de B. Taylor) (H-350k)...................................

Bach's Method of Trio-Playing. The 2-part Inventions, arranged as trios for two manuals and pedal, the third part added by Max Reger and Karl Straube. No. De-709 (not for U.S.A. and Canada)...

Chorale Preludes for Christmas: In dulci jubilo / Now sing we, now rejoice - Nun freut euch, liebe Christen g'mein / Now rejoice ye, beloved Christians - Nun komm', der Heiden Heiland / Come, Thou Saviour of the Gentiles - Vom Himmel hoch, da komm' ich her / From heaven above to earth I come (Fuga) - Wir Christenleut' hab'n jetzund Freud / We Christians may rejoice today - Der Tag, der ist so freudenreich / O day, so rich in gladness (P-2067d)..................

Musical Offering. The complete original edition with an Appendix containing (a) the Ricercare a 6 voci reduced to 2 or 3 staves for piano or organ, and (b) the Fuga Canonica arr. for Organ, or 2 or 3 players (P-219)...........................

Orgelbuechlein (Little Organ Book) (P-3946)...

Preludes, Fugues, Fantasias (P-4584)...

Short Preludes and Fugues (eight) (P-4442)...

(d) Organ Vocal Score and Figured Bass Bach Studies:

Christmas Oratorio. The Vocal Parts, with Organ either as the sole accompaniment or together with such parts of a Full Orchestra as may be available. For use with all current 'Christmas Oratorio' editions, and playable on a moderate-sized 3- (or even 2-) manual organ, adapted by Marmaduke P. Conway and Robert S. Munns (P-7031a)...

Schemelli's Musikalisches Gesangbuch of 1736. The 69 Sacred Songs and Arias, selected from " Schemelli " are among the most beautiful of religious music. They offer the greatest possible inspiration to those who are working on the realisation of figured bass. The melodies are printed in the tenor clef and the basses left just as Bach wrote them. Most suitable for practice beside the mechanical exercises offered in text-books (P-4573)..................................

BACH FACSIMILES

Bach Bicentenary Calendar, with Reproductions of Paintings and Drawings of Bach and his Family, with Facsimile Examples from their Compositions, several published for the first time. No. H-502.

Brandenburg Concertos. The six. The Autograph of the Brandenburg Concertos is regarded as one of the finest manuscripts of J. S. Bach which have come down to us. It is the dedication copy, sent by Bach in 1721 to the Margrave Christian Ludwig of Brandenburg - from whom the Brandenburg Concertos took their name. The MS. is in the possession of the Deutsche Staatsbibliothek in Berlin and was first issued in facsimile form for the Bach Memorial Year 1950. It is now available in a second Edition de luxe. No. P-7006.

Fantasia super ' Veni sancte spiritus ' (Come, Holy Ghost), in Facsimile, with Bach Portrait and Critical Analysis *by Peter Wackernagel.* No. De-117.

Inventions (two- and three-part), prefaced *by Ralph Kirkpatrick.* " The study of the Facsimile of this MS. is one of the greatest music lessons of a life-time." (*Musical America*). No. P-4201a.

Violoncello Solo Suites. Numbered edition, two parts in one cover, in the size of the original. Facsimile of the complete MS. together with an engraved (un-edited) edition. No. De-12.

ENGLISH BOOKS ON BACH

Art (The) of J. S. Bach. A comprehensive study *by A. E. F. Dickinson,* with many musical and pictorial Illustrations, a Glossary, Bibliography, Index to the music discussed, and a Numerical List of the Choral Cantatas, also classified according to the Church Year. Second enlarged edition. No. S-13.

Articulation in Organ-Playing, including a 'Little Organ Book for Manuals only', based on 31 Chorale Preludes and Chorales by Bach, in the order of the Liturgical Year with Commentaries on the Chorale Preludes and Chorales, and on the performance of the Chorales, with Ornamentation Examples (*Gordon Phillips*). *Foreword by R. Donington.* No. H-1001

Bach Biography (A short), *by Esther Meynell.* No. De-121.

Bach's Musical Structure. A 50-page study. Contained in " Challenge to Musical Tradition " *by A. T. Katz.* No. H-382.

Bach's Organ-Registration, *by William L. Sumner.* With *Foreword by Ivor Keys.* The German Organ in Bach's Time - The Nature of the Stops in the Organs played by Bach - The Use of the Divisions of the Organ - Pro Organo Pleno - Doppio Pedale - The young Bach's Expert Advice - Ein' feste Burg - The Tremulant - The Cymbelstern - Phrasing and Touch - Some accounts of Organ-registration in the 17th and early 18th Centuries - Stops in Bach's Organs - The Compasses of Bach's Organs. Also:
Bach's Chorale Prelude Titles in German and English, and
The BWV Numbering, and
The Nicknamed Organ Compositions. No. H-1002.

Organ (The) of Bach and **Gottfried Silbermann, Organ Builder,** *by William L. Sumner;* **The Organ Music of Bach,** *by Albert Riemenscheider and Herman Keller.* Including also: A Grading System - Bach Organ Recital Syllabus - Bach's Clavier Music - 45 Organ Specifications incl. those of every Organ on which J. S. B. is said to have played. Contained in Hinrichsen's Eighth Music Book. No. H-1956.

Samuel Wesley's Famous Bach Letters (1808-1816), and related Matters. Various Portraits and Facsimiles. Third (enlarged) edition. No. H-1958b.

Tempo and Rhythm in Bach's Organ Music, *by Robert Donington.* With *Foreword by Gordon Phillips.* Tempo as a Performer's Responsibility - Time Signatures - Words of Tempo - Fluctuations of Tempo - Conventions. No. H-1003.

GERMAN BOOKS ON BACH

Bach Congress 1950 in Leipzig. With Contributions by numerous international Bach Scholars, among them *D. Bartha, H. Besseler, W. Blankenburg, S. Borris, M. Dehnert, H. H. Draeger, A. Duerr, H. H. Eggebrecht, E. Flade, W. Gurlitt, K. Laux, Jos. Marx, E. H. Meyer, F. Oberborbeck, W. Schmieder, E. Schmitz, W. Serauky, D. Shostakovich, H. Sievers, W. Vetter, etc.* No. De-675.

Bachs Leben, Kunst und Kunstwerke, *by J. N. Forkel,* with a Portrait and 18 Musical Examples. Facsimile print from the first edition (published in 1802 in the Peters Edition). No. De-112.

Bachs Weltliche Kantaten. A musicological survey of the secular Cantatas, *by Ian Finlay.* No. De-119.

Der Thomaskantor. A study with numerous Illustrations, *by A. Strube.* No. De-686.

Die Klavier-Werke Bachs. Ein Beitrag zu ihrer Geschichte, Form, Deutung und Wiedergabe, *by Hermann Keller,* with many musical Illustrations. No. P-4571.

Die Orgel-Werke Bachs. A contribution to the History, Form, Interpretation and Performance of Bach's Organ Works, *by Hermann Keller.* A book of reference for the performer and student of Bach's Organ Works. Many musical Illustrations. No. P-4572.

Goethe's Relationship to Bach, *by Friedrich Smend.* No. De-680.

WILLIAM L. SUMNER'S
MUSICAL LITERARY WORK

apart from many Papers in English and American
Music Journals

A. THE ORGAN

Its Evolution, Principles of Construction and Use

Macdonald, London

B. THE ORGAN OF BACH
together with
GOTTFRIED SILBERMANN, ORGAN BUILDER

comprising Part One of Hinrichsen's Eighth Music Book

C. BACH'S ORGAN-REGISTRATION
(AND RELATED MATTERS)

with Foreword by Ivor Keys

Hinrichsen Edition No. 1002

D. FATHER WILLIS, ORGAN BUILDER AND HIS SUCCESSORS

Musical Opinion, London

E. THE PARISH CHURCH ORGAN

The Royal School of Chrch Music

F. CONTRIBUTIONS TO HINRICHSEN'S MUSIC BOOK SERIES

Acoustical Information and Statistics of Use to Musicians (Vol. II/III)
- Bach, The Organ of (VIII) - Bell Music (VI/V) - Cembal d'Amour,
The (VIII) - English Organ, The Present Development of the (II/III) -
French Organ School, The (VI) - Great Britain, Principal Organs in
(II/III) - Music and Science (I) - Musical Pitch, A History of (VII) -
Organ Music at the Royal Festival Hall (X) - Silbermann, Gottfried
(VIII) - Some Notes on Sweelinck (VIII).

ORGAN WORKS

with
historical-biographical Introductions and some Organ Specifications
Annotation and Registration Suggestions

By William L. Sumner

A. ORGAN ALBUMS

1. **Liszt: Shorter Organ Works:** Ave Maria by Arcadelt, Introitus, Ora pro nobis, Angelus. - Liszt as a Composer of Organ Music; Liszt's 4 major Organ Compositions; The Liszt Organ at Merseburg Cathedral; Comments on the Organ Compositions in this Volume (H-1043).......

2. **Mozart: Compositions for Organ,** with an Essay on Mozart's Work for Organ, Specifications of numerous Organs on which Mozart played, Annotation and Registration Suggestions........
   – Vol. 1. The Text and K.399 and K.546 supplemented by ' The Prague Improvisation', the latter edited by Ludwig Altman (H-1041a)........
   – Vol. 2. Three Pieces for Mechanical Organ, supplemented by some simpler versions (H-1041b)........

(to be continued)

B. FAMOUS ORGAN COMPOSITIONS

Vol. 1   **Böhm** (1661-1733): Praeludium and Fugue in C (P-4301d)........

Vol. 2   **Bruhns** (1665-1697): Praeludium and Fugue in E m. (P-4301q)........

Vol. 3   **Krebs** (1713-1780): Fugue in G, and reproduction of the one and only Bach relic (P-4301g)........

Vol. 4   **Liszt** (1811-1886): A Short Organ Mass (easy): Kyrie, Gloria, Graduale, Credo, Offertorium, Sanctus, Benedictus, Agnus Dei (P-1044)........

Vol. 5   **Mendelssohn** (1809-1847): Sonata Op. 65 No. 2 in C m. (P-1744c)........

Vol. 6   **Pachelbel** (1653-1706): Toccata and Fugue in C (P-4301h)........

Vol. 7   **Schubert** (1797-1828): Organ Fugue in E m. (P-4301k)........

Vol. 8   **Sweelinck** (1562-1621): " Mein junges Leben hat ein Ende / My Young Life hath an End." 6 Variations for Manuals only (P-4301c)

Vol. 9   **Sweelinck** (1562-1621) and **Scheidt** (1587-1654): " Est-ce Mars?" and the joint composition " Pavane Hispanica " (P-4301m)........

Vol. 10   **Sweelinck:** Echo Fantasie (P-4301n)........

Vol. 11   **Titelouze** (1563-1633): Pange lingua gloriosi. The Passion Hymn, with the complete Hymn by St. Thomas Aquinas (1227-1274) in Latin, English and German (P-4301e)........

Vol. 12   **Walther** (1684-1748): " Meinen Jesum lass' ich nicht / I will not forsake my Jesus". Chorale-Partita with the Chorale as harmonised by J. S. Bach, together with the original German and English words of its 6 Verses (P-4301p)........

(to be continued)

C. CHORALE PRELUDES ANCIENT AND MODERN

Some outstanding Examples of Organ Compositions based on
well-known Tunes
with historical-biographical Introductions and some Organ
Specifications Annotation and Registration Suggestions
by William L. Sumner.

(to be continued)

DATE DUE

OCT 1 2 1979			
NOV 2 2 1984			